PROBLEM BEHAVIOUR IN PEOPLE WITH SEVERE LEARNING DISABILITIES:
A Practical Guide to a Constructional Approach

PROBLEM BEHAVIOUR

IN PEOPLE WITH SEVERE LEARNING DISABILITIES

A Practical Guide to a Constructional Approach

EWA ZARKOWSKA AND JOHN CLEMENTS
Department of Clinical Psychology,
Institute of Psychiatry,
London

CROOM HELM
London & Sydney

© 1988 Ewa Zarkowska and John Clements
Croom Helm Ltd, Provident House,
Burrell Row, Beckenham, Kent BR3 1AT
Croom Helm Australia, 44–50 Waterloo Road,
North Ryde, 2113, New South Wales

British Library Cataloguing in Publication Data

Zarkowska, Ewa
   Problem behaviour in people with severe
   learning disabilities : a practical guide to
   a constructional approach.
   1. Learning disabilities   2. Behaviour
   modification
   I. Title   II. Clements, John
   371.9′043   LC4704
   ISBN 0-7099-3014-3

Distributed exclusively in the USA and non-exclusively in Canada by
Paul H. Brookes Publishing Co., Post Office Box 10624, Baltimore,
Maryland 21285–0624.

Filmset by Mayhew Typesetting, Bristol, England
Printed and bound in Great Britain by Mackays of Chatham Ltd, Kent

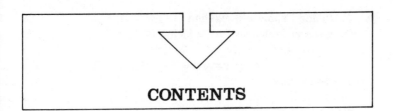

CONTENTS

Acknowledgements

Introduction

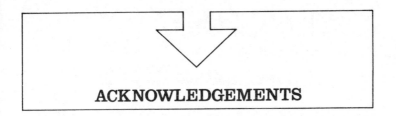

ACKNOWLEDGEMENTS

Our grateful thanks to Jean Morgan for her secretarial assistance in the preparation of this manuscript, and to Bogdan Zarkowski, who provided the graphics for this book.

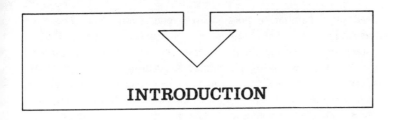

INTRODUCTION

This book is about the management of the behaviour problems of adults and children who have severe learning disabilities. It is intended to be a practical guide for those involved in the daily care, education and training of clients with severe learning problems, to help them analyse and deal effectively with the behavioural challenges posed by their clients. More specifically, the aims of this book are:

(1) to describe a systematic method of assessing problem behaviours;
(2) to present a step-by-step guide to planning high-quality intervention strategies;
(3) to describe methods for implementing high-quality programmes of behaviour change;
(4) to describe methods of protecting the rights of learning disabled clients against misuse/abuse of behaviour-management procedures;
(5) to describe methods of supporting staff in their endeavours to implement and sustain programmes of behaviour change.

The approach described here is derived from the authors' extensive experience of problem behaviour management in a variety of day and residential settings (including Hilda Lewis House, a specialist assessment and treatment unit for children and young people with severe learning and behavioural difficulties). It is based on their wide practical experience of training staff from various professional disciplines in the principles and techniques of behaviour management. It is a multidimensional approach in which the analysis of behaviour problems takes place at several levels. Such an analysis leads to a number of possible intervention strategies. These are determined by the nature of the problem, the individual characteristics of the client, the environment in which the problem occurs, and the resources available for dealing with the problem.

Each level at which assessment and intervention can take place is described in a separate section of the book. We have tried to make the sections as self-contained as possible so that the reader can more easily use this as a reference book when planning and implementing different aspects of a programme of behaviour change. However, there is some cross-referencing between sections to avoid unnecessary repetition of details.

Section One presents an overview of the approach that is taken, discussing its theoretical, philosophical and practical perspectives. Section Two deals with the broad issue of assessment and the planning of a comprehensive management strategy based on the assessment. Section Three describes how to translate the management plan into specific goals for intervention. In Section Four procedures for teaching new skills relevant to the long-term resolution of a problem behaviour are described, and in Section Five techniques for encouraging important existing skills are presented. Methods of tackling problem behaviours more directly are described in Section Six. Section Seven considers methods which can be used to encourage the individual to manage his own behaviour and in Section Eight procedures for monitoring and evaluating progress are outlined. In contrast to the client-oriented focus of these sections, Section Nine discusses the broader issues involved in the management of severe behaviour problems. These are issues of organisational support and client protection.

The approach described here is a complex one, reflecting the complex nature of the behaviour problems of people who have severe learning disabilities and the challenge which these problems present to those charged with their care. It is unlikely that the individual reader acting alone will be able to carry out all aspects of the work that may be necessary for the long-term resolution of a problem behaviour. For this, a team effort may be required, and the reader should bear this in mind when using this text.

The work involved at each level requires a thorough understanding of the principles involved. We have therefore, as far as possible, divided each section into two parts. The first describes the general principles involved in interventions at that level, and the second part is a more practical step-by-step guide to planning and intervening at that level.

Before embarking on the text, a brief explanation needs to be given about the terminology that will be used. The people with whom this book is concerned are referred to in every-day language and professional jargon by a variety of labels: for example, mentally handicapped, or moderately, severely or profoundly retarded. These labels arise for historical reasons and have changed many times over the years. More recently a distinction has been drawn between the intellectual impairment that affects these people, the severe learning disability that arises out of this impairment, and the resulting handicaps or disadvantages that may prevent the individual fulfilling a normal role in society. If a general label is to be used, therefore, it seems more appropriate to refer to people who have an intellectual impairment or learning disability rather than people who are handicapped or retarded. Handicaps are as much determined by opportunities and lack of opportunities as by the severity of the learning disability itself. In this book, therefore, we will refer to people with intellectual or learning impairments and disabilities, rather than 'mentally handicapped' or 'retarded'.

When describing our approach to the management of problem behaviours of people with learning disabilities, we refer to them sometimes as clients and sometimes as students: clients, because they are the recipients of a service that is being provided for them; students, because, in the context of the approach adopted, they often need to be taught new skills or alternative ways of responding. In this sense, they are indeed students. In a similar vein, caregivers are frequently referred to as teachers — this being a role they must adopt when tackling problem behaviours from the perspective presented here.

Finally, we are aware of referring to our clients and students in the masculine gender throughout the text. This has been done purely for practical reasons and not in any way out of prejudice or discrimination.

1

AN APPROACH TO THE UNDERSTANDING AND MANAGEMENT OF BEHAVIOUR PROBLEMS

IDENTIFYING BEHAVIOUR PROBLEMS

The presence of a behaviour problem is not always a clear-cut matter. A person may have been acting in a particular way for a considerable time before anyone decides to call that action 'a problem'. Alternatively, there may be several people behaving in a similar way, but only one is identified as having a problem. Thus, this apparently simple decision appears to be a complex judgement determined by the behaviour of the person, the behaviour of those around him and the beliefs, attitudes and feelings of the person making the judgement. This state of affairs is compounded by a tendency to place together people with learning disabilities and separate them from others of a similar age. As a result, both the people with these difficulties and those who work with them become isolated from the mainstream of society. In such circumstances it is easy to develop routines, expectations and standards which may be inappropriate for the age and developmental level of the individual, or standards which are designed to assist in the smooth running of the institution but which are quite at variance with the needs of the individual client (for example, setting an 8.00 p.m. bedtime for adult clients simply because night staff arrive on duty at 8.30 p.m. and a hand-over time is needed). Such problems are not confined to large institutions. They can also occur in small-group care settings and even in natural family settings.

Inappropriate standards and expectations are particularly evident in work with adolescents and young adults. Like others at that age, people with learning problems may become moody, defiant and resentful of authority when they reach adolescence. They may become able to articulate their own opinions, thoughts and feelings more clearly and start to stand up for themselves and their rights. In the normal course of events, adults learn to accommodate to these developments. They reduce the number of demands, learn to qualify instructions with explanations of why these should be carried out, and give the individual more space, decision-making responsibility and financial independence. These adaptations often do not take place in the development of the person with learning disabilities, partly because people with learning impairments and those who work with them are isolated from the mainstream of society, so that they may be unaware of what the 'norm' should be; and partly also because of the conflicting cues presented by people with severe learning problems. Physically and emotionally they may 'act their age' but their level of understanding and ability to articulate is much more limited and is characteristic of a younger age. This is an important issue to face, as many behaviour problems in adolescence and young adulthood arise when demands are made upon the individual or when the individual's expression of a wish or preference is denied.

Before attempting to change the behaviour of someone who has severe learning disabilities it is important, therefore, to consider whether a 'problem' behaviour is indeed a problem for the individual or whether it is more a problem for the setting in which he finds himself. The answer to that question is not always a simple one. Nevertheless it clearly has important implications for any programme of change since it may be that in some cases the answer will be to change the inappropriate practices and routines rather than the behaviour of the individual. The following guidelines, while not resolving all the issues that arise, may help to make this initial important decision. A behaviour may legitimately be regarded as a problem if it satisfies some or all of the following criteria:

(1) The behaviour itself or its severity is inappropriate given a person's age and level of development.
(2) The behaviour is dangerous either to the person himself or to others.
(3) The behaviour constitutes a significant additional handicap for the person by interfering with the learning of new skills or by excluding the person from important learning opportunities.
(4) The behaviour causes significant stress to the lives of those who live and work with the person, and impairs the quality of their lives to an unreasonable degree.
(5) The behaviour is contrary to social norms.

If it is clear, using the above criteria, that a behaviour is indeed a problem for the individual, then, provided that consent is first obtained either from the individual or those representing him, ways need to be found to help him overcome that problem.

UNDERSTANDING PROBLEM BEHAVIOURS

Behavioural difficulties present a serious and continuing challenge to those who live and work with people who have learning impairments. The incidence of significant behaviour problems among this group is considerably higher than in the general population. According to some estimates, as many as 50–60% of people who have learning impairments are likely also to present with a significant behaviour disorder. Many of these problem behaviours are similar to those which may be found in the general population (for example, tantrums, aggression, absconding or screaming), but there are also other kinds of behaviours less commonly found in the general population (repetitive behaviours such as rocking, finger flicking; socially inappropriate and age-inappropriate behaviours such as over-friendliness to strangers, stripping or soiling; ritualistic behaviours such as clinging to objects, insisting on specific routines and, occasionally, more distressing self-injurious behaviours such as self-hitting, self-biting or eye poking).

There is often a tendency to use rather simple models to interpret such behaviours. People with learning and behavioural difficulties may be seen as 'sick' (passive, ignorant, in need of expert care), 'dangerous' (irrational, untrustworthy, violent, in need of control and supervision), 'perpetual children' (not developing, needing to be indulged at times but directed on all important matters). Such simplistic models reflect a lack of understanding for the special problems and needs of this group. In fact, it is unusual to find a single or direct cause of behavioural difficulties. There are, however, a number of factors which may contribute to the presence of behaviour problems and which may explain their high incidence among people with severe learning disabilities. None of these factors is exclusive to people with learning impairments, and, when present among people of normal intellectual ability, they are also associated with a greater likelihood of a person's having a behaviour problem.

In the first place there are a number of *biological* factors that can increase the likelihood of a person's having a behaviour problem. Such factors include organic brain dysfunction, epilepsy, hearing and visual impairments and certain temperamental characteristics, such as a high intensity of emotional responding and poor adaptability to new situations. *Social* factors too have an important influence on behaviour. For example, people who receive poor quality institutional care, or who are rejected by society and by their peers, are more likely to develop a behaviour problem than are their contemporaries who do not experience these factors. Environments in which there is a high level of tension and interpersonal conflict are more likely to engender behaviour problems than ones where there is harmony and cohesion. Learning experiences, such as consistency in discipline and management, are also very important influences.

People with learning impairments often have a long history of failure in many areas of their lives. In addition, they frequently remain overdependent on others for their needs so that their self-concept may be quite poor. Such *emotional* factors can themselves be important determinants of behaviour. Finally, there are a number of important *cognitive* factors which have been associated with the occurrence of behaviour problems and which are frequently seen in people with learning impairments. These include poor problem-solving skills, poor communication skills and poor social skills.

Any of these factors — biological, social, emotional and cognitive — can influence behaviour, whatever a person's intellectual level. The more factors that occur together, the greater the likelihood of behaviour problems developing. Many people with learning disabilities are exposed to a large number of these influences, which are likely to interact with each other. Thus the determinants of behaviour problems among this group are likely to be many and they are likely also to be complex.

APPROACHES TO THE MANAGEMENT OF PROBLEM BEHAVIOURS

Approaches to the management of behaviour problems of people with severe learning disabilities have for the most part been quite narrowly focused and often influenced by people's own theoretical perspective. Thus, medical approaches have focused on the use of chemical interventions, for example to reduce anxiety or suppress agitation. Socially oriented approaches have emphasised the importance of high-quality 'normal' living environments, stressing the need to provide people with greater autonomy over their lives by allowing them more choices, greater privacy, their own belongings and their own personal space. Educational approaches have emphasised the importance of increasing people's repertoires of skills on the assumption that, in the absence of more appropriate responses, people will use whatever skills they have available to meet their various living needs. Behavioural approaches have stressed the role of learning, emphasising the importance of environmental factors in the maintenance of problem behaviours, in particular the consequences and antecedents of behaviour. They have developed techniques, largely based on contingent reinforcement and contingent punishment, for increasing appropriate skills and decreasing problem behaviours.

Given that problem behaviours are likely to be the result of a large number of interacting factors, it is not surprising that such narrowly focused approaches have, on the whole, been quite limited in their effectiveness. Chemical interventions, for example, while sometimes suppressing inappropriate behaviours, do not teach more appropriate ways of responding, so that problems can occur when medication is withdrawn. Similarly with social approaches: new and more appropriate ways of responding do not automatically appear when high-quality living environments are provided, so that in and of themselves they produce limited and short-term gains. The traditional behavioural approach, while providing reinforcing and punishing consequences for behaviours to inform the individual about their appropriateness and to increase his motivation to alter his behaviour, have not really focused on modifying setting conditions, which are the context in which problems may occur, nor on altering the more immediate triggers for problem behaviours. Thus, even this widely used approach to problem behaviour management, despite its sophisticated technology and the dramatic and rapid effects sometimes reported, has in practice often had only limited success. In particular, effects of interventions can be short-lived with problems recurring or new ones developing in their place. Changes in behaviour can be situation specific, that is, behavioural improvements obtained in one setting may not readily generalise to other places or people outside of the environment where training was conducted. Such limitations in treatment effectiveness have led behavioural scientists to look to ways of improving existing approaches and techniques.

Coupled with the recognition of the limitations of the traditional behavioural approach there has been a growing disinclination among behaviourists to use punishment techniques except in the most extreme cases, partly because professional attitudes towards people with learning disabilities have changed in favour of a more 'normalised' approach, and partly because there is now increasing evidence that changes in antecedent events, rather than just in the consequences for behaviour, can significantly contribute to behaviour change.

The approach described in this book reflects recent approaches to behaviour management. It is, essentially, an extension of the traditional behavioural approach which emphasises the importance of environmental factors in the understanding and treatment of behaviour problems but which, in common with educational approaches, shares the belief that the teaching of alternative skills is a crucial aspect of effective behaviour management. In common with socially oriented approaches, it shares the view that the physical and emotional environment in which a person finds himself has an important influence on behaviour, so that lasting behavioural change cannot occur without careful attention to the settings in which problems occur. It is thus a multicomponent approach which acknowledges and encompasses the many factors — social, cognitive, emotional and learning — which may be influencing a person's behaviour.

Within the approach described in this book the analysis of behaviour problems takes place at several levels. Interventions, too, are likely to need to be carried out at a number of levels. It is thus a broad problem-solving approach rather than a cook-book of ready-made treatment packages. It offers a framework for analysing and understanding problem behaviours and a framework for planning and implementing intervention strategies, while at the same time adhering to the rigid scientific methodology of the behavioural tradition, with its emphasis on efficiency, consistency and objectivity. The model presented is concerned with four essential factors: settings, triggers, actions, results. Analysis of behaviour problems and interventions take place at these four levels. To help the reader keep these four factors in mind during the assessment of a problem behaviour and when planning intervention programmes, we have called this the STAR model.

THE STAR MODEL OF BEHAVIOUR MANAGEMENT

Analysing problem behaviours

The STAR model for analysing and managing problem behaviours of people with severe learning disabilities does not concern itself with abstract causal inferences about problem behaviours. According to this model it is less useful, for example, to understand a person's ritualistic or obsessional behaviours in terms of his 'autism' than to understand the circumstances in which these behaviours occur and the consequences that result for the individual by performing these actions. This latter information is more likely to be helpful for devising intervention programmes. Abstract factors may be difficult to pinpoint. In addition, factors that may have been involved in the genesis of a problem behaviour may be quite different from factors that are maintaining that behaviour months or years after it first appeared. For example, a young child may have started to bang his head with his fists in response to an ear infection but may continue to bang once the infection has cleared, having learned that head banging can be an effective means of gaining attention or of getting out of unpleasant situations. Thus, historical causal inferences about behaviours are often not helpful for developing intervention programmes. Rather, behaviour problems of people with severe learning disabilities are more usefully understood in terms of the four STAR factors: settings, triggers, actions, results. These factors are also the key elements in the management of behaviour problems.

Settings

Settings are the stable, or relatively stable, features of the environment in which actions occur. For example, the setting for sleeping is, generally, the bedroom. The classroom or workplace is usually the setting for attending to instructions and working. Being tired or unwell is often the setting in which the person shows irritable behaviours. Disrupted routines may be the setting in which some individuals become anxious. Settings can be composed of any of a large number of factors: places, people, times, tension in the environment, hunger, and so on. They are the general context in which actions are performed.

Triggers

Triggers are the signals that are present within settings which 'set off' specific actions in a given situation. For example, the light being turned off in the bedroom is the trigger for a child to close his eyes to go to sleep. The alarm clock ringing is the trigger for an individual to wake up. The red traffic light acts as a trigger for the driver to apply his foot to the brake. Triggers can 'set off' actions, or they can be the signal to stop ongoing activities. Triggers gain control over actions because they have been consistently associated with specific results during learning and inform the individual that a pleasant result is achievable or that an unpleasant result may be imminent.

Actions

Actions are observable behaviours. They can be new skills which need to be learned, unacceptable behaviours which need to be reduced, or existing skills which need to be encouraged. Actions are affected by environmental variables. In other words, they are determined by the settings in which a person finds himself, they are 'set off' by specific triggers, and they achieve some kind of result for the individual.

Results

Results are the events that follow an action. They provide information about the appropriateness of that action and also serve as motivators which encourage or discourage a person from performing an action again. There are two classes of results which can follow an action: reinforcers and punishers. *Reinforcers* increase the likelihood that an action will be performed again: in other words, they strengthen or encourage behaviour. *Positive reinforcement* occurs when an individual's action is followed by something pleasant: a gain (for example, smiles, attention, special treats, money). *Negative reinforcement* occurs when an action is followed by the cessation of something unpleasant: in other words, escape (for example, being left alone, getting out of doing a difficult task). *Punishers* decrease the likelihood that an action will be performed in the future: in other words, punishers serve to weaken or discourage behaviour. Being admonished, being hurt, being deprived of privileges or attention can all act as punishers.

According to the STAR model, problem behaviours are skills. Like any skills they are learned and, to a large extent, maintained by the results they achieve for the individual. Results may include attention, sympathy, material gains or escape from unpleasant or difficult situations. To give some examples, if a young child who likes people and their attention finds that every time he uses the potty, people praise, clap and show signs of delight, then he is more likely to try to use the potty in the future. If a person with learning disabilities screams when asked to do some unpleasant task and is thereby left alone, it is more likely that he will scream when asked to do this task in the future.

Actions are rarely performed on a random basis. People are very efficient at knowing which behaviours are appropriate in a given situation. This is because, in the course of learning, they find that their actions, whether acceptable or unacceptable, achieve looked-for results in some settings and not in others. For example, a child may learn that if he screams at home in the presence of his mother, this may give him access to sweets or drinks or get him out of going to bed on time. That same behaviour at school, however, may simply be ignored by his teacher and not achieve any positive outcomes for him. Such experiences allow people to predict the situations in which specific actions are likely to be appropriate or effective. Within these settings, however, there are a host of stimuli which come to act as triggers that 'set off' these actions, because they remind the individual that the looked-for result is imminent. Thus the sight of the sweet counter in the supermarket might 'set off' a temper tantrum; a verbal instruction 'Come here' might 'set off' an appropriate approach response.

There are other less obvious setting and trigger factors that are important for the understanding and management of behaviour problems. Some 'problem' behaviours, for example, are triggered by factors such as fear, anger or anxiety. The settings that give rise to these may be many and varied. For example, conflict between family members at home may give rise to a state of anxiety within the individual; being teased or being denied the freedom to make choices in a situation may give rise to anger; being faced with an aversive object or situation may give rise to fear; being presented with a number of surprising or exciting events may give rise to a general state of arousal. These states are accompanied by many physiological changes within the body: increased heart rate, sweatiness, muscle tension. This may be tolerated by the individual up to a certain level, but once a level is reached which can no longer be tolerated, this may act as a trigger for problem behaviours. Settings and triggers are important to the understanding and management of problem behaviours as are the results which these actions achieve.

9

Managing problem behaviours

Replacing problem behaviours with appropriate skills

Problem behaviours should be regarded as purposeful actions which are directed at achieving specific results. As such, they serve an important function for the individual: they may be a means of communicating that the individual wants attention or help or that a situation is unacceptable. They may be a means of protesting against an imposed unpleasant event, or they may be a means of occupation or stimulation. For this reason, simply trying to reduce or remove an unacceptable action is unlikely to provide a lasting solution since the individual may be left with no appropriate alternative skill by which to achieve the same goals. Lasting solutions to resolving behaviour problems are more likely to be achieved if appropriate skills that can replace the unwanted behaviour are taught or encouraged. Such skills are likely to be ones that can serve the same function for the individual as the problem behaviour: for example, a more appropriate means of protesting or communicating the unacceptability of a situation or of obtaining stimulation. Alternatively, they may be skills that are physically incompatible with that behaviour. It is useful to teach or encourage physically incompatible skills because, while performing these, an individual cannot simultaneously be performing the unacceptable action.

Teaching and encouraging alternative skills requires careful attention to STAR factors: settings, which create optimal conditions for learning and skill practice; triggers, which can 'set off' performance of appropriate skills; and results which serve to motivate the individual to learn and practise alternative responses and inform him of their appropriateness.

Modifying settings in which problem behaviours occur

Great emphasis is placed on the emotional and physical environment in which problem behaviours occur. These factors are important not just for the understanding of behaviour problems but also for their treatment. Thus, temporary or permanent changes may need to be made either within the physical environment (increasing stimulation, allowing greater autonomy, relaxing rules) or within the emotional environment (modifying settings which provoke anxiety or stress, treating depression or fears).

Modifying triggers that set off problem behaviours

If clear and circumscribed triggers can be identified as reliably 'setting off' problem behaviours, then interventions may usefully be carried out at this level. Triggers may sometimes be removed permanently. Or they may be removed temporarily, and gradually reintroduced in a way that avoids the problem behaviour's occurring. For example, if the appearance of a particular person (trigger) within the classroom (setting) consistently 'sets off' inappropriate attention-seeking behaviour, then that person might initially be removed from the setting, then gradually phased back in a way which does not allow the opportunity for an inappropriate response, while at the same time ensuring that appropriate behaviour in the presence of that person leads to a result which is positively reinforcing for the individual. By teaching the individual that in the presence of this person certain appropriate actions lead to positive results, that person will in time become a trigger for appropriate behaviours and cease to be a trigger for inappropriate ones.

Removing or altering results achieved by problem behaviours

When a problem behaviour is consistently and regularly performed, it must be assumed that it achieves positive results for the individual at least on some occasions. Part of the overall intervention strategy will therefore need to focus on the results attained by the problem behaviour — to ensure that looked-for results do not occur following an unacceptable action and, in extreme cases, to provide an unpleasant result each time the behaviour occurs in order to discourage its performance while more appropriate skills are being taught and encouraged.

Encouraging self-management

Programmes of behaviour change are likely to involve a high level of external control over the individual. This may not always be necessary, desirable or even feasible. Within all aspects of the individual's programme, therefore, consideration needs to be given to the possibility of involving the client in the management of his own behaviour: to record his own actions, to provide reinforcement for his appropriate behaviours or take control over triggers that 'set off' his inappropriate actions. Such involvement increases the individual's control over his environment and may enhance his commitment to his programme of change.

Using arbitrary STAR factors

In the early stages of behaviour change, *arbitrary* STAR factors may need to be introduced to accelerate learning. Arbitrary settings, triggers and results are ones which would not naturally be present or occur when a given action is performed but which have been added deliberately to make learning easier. Thus artificial environments may be used in the early stages of skill learning to create the optimal conditions for learning (for example, individual sessions in a special teaching area); arbitrary triggers, in the form of prompts and reminders, may be used to accelerate learning; and arbitrary results, in the form of special reinforcers or contrived punishers, may serve to increase motivation for behaviour change.

Using a graded approach

In order to increase the opportunity for clients to learn new skills and to facilitate consistency in management, it is important to adopt a graded approach to change. A graded approach increases the likelihood of progress occurring and of progress being seen both by the client and by his care givers. The experience of progress is an important motivator for both care staff and clients and helps them persist with their long-term efforts at behaviour change. Thus long-term goals are broken down into small achievable steps and practised one step at a time. Programmes for managing problem behaviours are often introduced gradually — first in one setting during specific sessions, then systematically extended across settings and time. New skills are taught in stages — first one part of the skill, then another. A graded approach makes learning for the client easier and it eases the workload for staff. It therefore has many advantages.

Providing efficient teaching

The fundamental difficulty experienced by people with learning impairments is their difficulty in learning. They therefore cannot afford to have teachers who are inefficient, who are unclear about the aims and methods of their programmes or who change their teaching from day to day. For this reason, great emphasis is placed on efficiency in order that behaviour change may occur as quickly as possible.

To carry out a programme of behaviour change efficiently requires *precision* at a number of levels. In the first place it is important to be precise about behaviours which are the focus of interest, so that people are in no doubt about the actions they are attempting to analyse and change. This may not be quite as straightforward as it may seem. In everyday language people often describe themselves and others by referring to inner states and processes such as feelings, beliefs or attitudes which are not visible to the outside observer. In judging other people, actions are often interpreted as indicating something going on inside the person, something which cannot actually be seen. Thus, if a person looks serious, talks sharply to others, sighs loudly and slams doors, he may be said to be in a bad mood. However, whereas the facial expression, the verbal behaviour, the breathing pattern and the shutting of doors can be observed, the 'mood' cannot be seen. People talk as if all the behaviours are part of the same thing (the mood) which is the inner unobservable state. In the same way, people are described as being angry, jealous, sociable, bad tempered. It is a very common way of talking and understanding other people.

This natural way of talking about people presents us with some difficulties. Inferences about others are very much influenced by people's own feelings and beliefs. If a person is feeling sad, he may only notice the negative things that other people do and is more likely to see in their behaviour feelings of hostility or rejection towards himself. Thus different people may make different judgements on the basis of seeing the same thing. If two people observe a child snatching back a toy which has been snatched from him, one may see this as a sign of underlying insecurity, the other indicating appropriate assertiveness. Of course these two different interpretations will lead to very different kinds of response to the action. For this reason, all behaviours or 'inner states' must be defined in terms of observable actions. For example, anxiety might be defined in terms of pacing around a room, remaining seated at a task for no more than a few seconds, or clinging to other people. Actions must always be defined very precisely so that there can be no doubt in people's minds about the action in question, be it a skill to be learned or an inappropriate behaviour to be decreased.

A second level at which *precision* is required concerns the aims and methods of intervention. If the goals of programmes are left unstated or are stated imprecisely, this can lead to ambiguity and differences in interpretation. Thus there may be disagreement about whether goals have been achieved, particularly when several people are involved. To avoid this happening, the aims of each programme of change are always specified in precise terms.

The same applies to methods of intervention. If different people try to teach a skill to a single client, each using a different approach, or different people try to decrease an inappropriate action using different techniques, then clients may become confused about what is expected of them. This happens because they receive contradictory messages from caregivers who provide different amounts of help, correct errors in different ways or consequate actions using a variety of methods. *Consistency* is an important aspect of an efficient approach to management. To this end, written plans and programme details form an essential component of behaviour management.

Written programmes serve a number of functions. Having to write them out is an aid to clear thinking and helps avoid time wasted through forgetting to plan for certain events (for example, planning what materials to have available). Given that the STAR approach involves detailed planning, written programmes decrease the load on memory and help caregivers to maintain a consistent approach. They also serve to improve communication and consistency where several different people are to be involved in a programme of change. The presence of a written plan, especially if posted up in an obvious place, may also act as a reminder to carry out a programme. This may be particularly important when working with people who have very severe learning disabilities or where staff are under considerable pressure to do a range of other things. Too often people with learning impairments are unable to 'remind' those who work with them of their learning needs. Too often carrying out teaching and management programmes is one of many demands upon staff. A written programme is a reminder of the importance of this activity. It also serves to document a learning history for the person with learning disabilities. Through the accumulation of written programmes, much insight can be gained into the general characteristics of the learner: which skills are mastered more easily, which methods work more effectively. Such a history is an essential means for developing an efficient, individually based approach to behaviour management.

A further important reason for written programmes relates to the protection of the individual's human rights. Programmes for unacceptable behaviours may include an aversive component and may sometimes require physically or socially intrusive interventions. It is essential to protect the person's rights when using such strategies. A written programme is a document which is open to scrutiny and, as such, is likely to encourage people to consider all its ethical implications before implementing it.

Maintaining objectivity

When carrying out programmes of behaviour change, it is important to know whether or not progress is occurring, how quickly or slowly it is happening and when aims have been achieved. This information is very important when making decisions about adapting, changing or even abandoning programmes so that time is not wasted persisting with programmes which do not work or continuing unchanged with programmes once success has been achieved. This, again, may not be as simple as it may seem. Judgements about progress which are based on subjective assessments and on people's recall of how things were before a programme was started are likely to be influenced by a number of things. First of all, people tend to recall events which are emotionally charged and which stand out from the norm. They are therefore more likely to remember a single unacceptable behaviour than the hundreds of appropriate responses that an individual performs during the day. Thus a judgement of 'no progress' can easily be made shortly after an unpleasant action has occurred, even though it may be several days since a previous incident took place. Judgements about progress are influenced also by people's own feelings at the time of making the judgement. If a person is tired, unwell or unhappy, he is less likely to be tolerant of the inappropriate behaviours of others than on a day when he is feeling energetic and optimistic. As a result his impressions of a client's progress are likely to be influenced by his own mood or feelings, which will fluctuate from time to time. For these reasons objective records of progress are an important part of an efficient system of behaviour management. Record keeping is important for other reasons too. Some interventions (see Section Six) may lead to an initial increase in a problem behaviour before it begins to decrease. It may take time to find an appropriate intervention procedure suited to the individual, and several different approaches may have to be tried. Only if there are objective records can such choices be made on an accurate basis. Records do not, however, just provide *information*. They also provide *motivation*. A visible record of progress may be a source of encouragement to both student and teacher alike. Objective record keeping, which consists of a formal system of data collection, is thus an integral part of the STAR system.

Facilitating constructive interventions

Effective and lasting solutions to behaviour problems are more likely to occur when interventions are carried out across a number of dimensions: changing settings or triggers, removing or otherwise altering results for problem behaviours, building up existing skills, and/or teaching relevant new skills. The management of behaviour problems is therefore likely to be a long-term undertaking. In particular, new skills which may need to be mastered may take months, in some cases years, to learn. Programmes of change or some of their components, at least, may need to be sustained over long periods of time. A graded approach means they will need to be reviewed and modified regularly and frequently. In addition, they may need to be carried out in a number of different environments. The importance of these aspects of behaviour management is frequently underscored. Effective management of behaviour problems requires more than an understanding of the principles and techniques involved. It also requires careful attention to organisational factors. Even the most skilled caregiver will have difficulty making a significant and lasting impact on a problem behaviour if the organisation within which change is to occur does not facilitate the time-consuming and detailed work required to effect change. This means providing time for planning, for writing programmes and for monitoring and evaluating change, and a forum for decision making and for reviewing progress. It means also a clear and positive value assigned to working with difficult clients so that staff can feel that their work is supported by the organisation.

In addition to these organisational factors, the importance of the influence of the working team also cannot be underestimated. Effective management of behaviour problems requires a consistent approach. Consistency across people and places is very important, never more so than in institutional, residential or day-care settings where a large number of people may be involved in the management of the individual. If consistency is to occur, there must be close co-operation among the people involved. This means working together as a team. Team work requires a unity of purpose, clear and effective communication between team members and a clear structure within which the work of the team can be conducted.

Just as attention needs to be paid to the organisation and the team carrying out programmes of change, so, too, attention must be paid to the client himself — his rights and interests in relation to the attempts and decisions of others to alter his behaviour. The needs of the client must at all times be balanced against the goals and methods of behaviour change. Again, this very important aspect of behaviour management can only be certain of the attention it requires in the context of a planned and structured organisational framework.

Within the STAR approach, the management of problem behaviour therefore takes place at two levels. At the first level, people must know and understand the principles and techniques of behaviour change. At the second level, the people who are to carry out programmes of change must be provided with an organisational structure within which the many aspects of their task can be facilitated, where teamwork can be encouraged and sustained and where the rights of the client can be protected.

SUMMARY

The management of behaviour problems in people who have learning disabilities is not a straightforward matter. There are no ready-made solutions. Rather, each person must be assessed individually, in the context of his own skills and in the context of the environments in which the problem occurs, so that strategies can be worked out which are best suited to that individual and which are feasible to carry out within the organisational set-up in which the problem occurs. There is unlikely to be just one 'correct' strategy. A number of alternative procedures may be equally effective.

In this book we present a framework within which a problem behaviour can be assessed and a broad framework for planning, implementing and evaluating intervention programmes. The approach is multidimensional and it is one that may require considerable time and manpower resources, particularly when problems are of a severe nature, in addition to careful attention to organisational issues. It may, therefore, prove difficult to implement the entire 'package' in certain settings, particularly where staffing levels are low. Nevertheless there are many levels at which change can take place and there are many ways of tackling problems at each level, such that certain aspects of the 'package' may be more easily implemented than others. In such cases, doing a little is better than doing nothing at all. Settings can often be improved or altered within existing structural frameworks. New skills can be taught by a single individual without the need for a full back-up organisational system. Existing skills can sometimes be encouraged informally without too much demand on resources. Tackling any of these components may reduce problems to some extent and should therefore be done, even if other components are more difficult to implement. The problem-solving approach presented in this book should thus provide the reader with a framework for analysing and tackling the behavioural challenges of his client in a way which is adapted both to the needs of the client and to the settings in which programmes of change need to be carried out.

ESTABLISHING
A MANAGEMENT PLAN

When a person is identified as having a behaviour problem for which help is required, the situation is often viewed with a sense of urgency and is seen as a crisis. This sense of crisis and urgency may induce people to try to alleviate the problem by adopting measures which often produce only short-term solutions and later recurrence of the problems. Even more unfortunately, the sense of urgency may encourage people to adopt measures which are not necessarily in the individual's best interests, for example the use of excessive

Figure 2.1

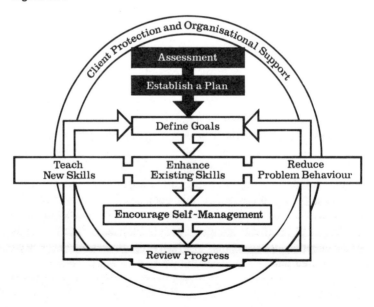

punishments or resorting to high doses of medication. It is a theme of this book that the effective management of behaviour problems in people with serious learning disabilities requires a long-term perspective. Behaviour problems cannot be understood in isolation but need to be considered in the context of the entire person and the world in which he lives. The ultimate resolution of a problem behaviour will depend on replacing inappropriate actions with other more appropriate skills and on changing those aspects of the environment which may be maintaining the problem behaviour. This requires a highly individualised approach. There is no instant recipe for managing specific problems. Thus, in order to devise an effective, individually-tailored management strategy, it is important first to carry out a comprehensive assessment of a person's skills, the problem behaviour and the environments in which the problem does and does not occur. A comprehensive assessment is an essential first step in planning an overall management strategy.

A. GENERAL PRINCIPLES FOR ESTABLISHING A MANAGEMENT PLAN

Assessing the problem behaviour

A full analysis of the problem will include an assessment of the settings that affect whether or not it occurs, an assessment of triggers that may 'set off' the problem behaviour, and an assessment of the results that the behaviour achieves for the individual (this should highlight the functions that the behaviour may serve for him).

Setting conditions and problem behaviours

There are a large number of setting factors that affect whether or not problem behaviours occur. One important range of setting factors relates to what is sometimes called 'atmosphere'. In particular, settings in which there is tension and conflict between people create the conditions where problem behaviours are likely to occur. This is true in family settings and in residential or day-care settings. Examples of such setting factors are marital stress between parents, a new teacher settling in at school, staff changes within a residential unit or even the school's preparation for the Christmas play. Another kind of 'atmosphere' factor which often relates to conflict is lack of purpose. Settings where staff are clear about why they are

19

there and what their goals are, are more likely to create conditions where progress is achieved than settings where people are uncertain about what they are trying to achieve with students and why they are trying to achieve it. In such settings the likelihood of problem behaviours is increased. This is a very common problem, particularly in work with older and very disabled people. A general philosophy and sense of purpose is an important setting condition within which specific programmes can flourish.

One particular condition which may be a source of stress and uncertainty of purpose is isolation from positive social contact and exposure to negative social contact. Thus, parents who have few sources of support, who are in conflict with their relatives, neighbours and welfare agencies, will have difficulty in managing their children and in coping with very specific programmes. The same problems can be seen in day or residential facilities which become isolated and subject to criticism.

Another group of setting conditions relates to *state* factors within the student. A person who has sleeping problems, for example, may show behaviour problems during the day. It is not always clear whether these problems are related, but certainly lack of sleep can make a person more irritable and more likely to behave in an un-acceptable way. Other sources of irritability are pain, hunger and thirst. These can be important factors in the occurrence of behaviour problems, particularly for people who have very limited communication skills, and should always be carefully checked. Another kind of state variable which can be important is depression. Depression in a psychiatric sense refers to a general lowering of mood with continual feelings of sadness and worthlessness. It may influence appetite, sleep, level of social interaction, energy level and general irritability. People with severe learning problems can get depressed, but again their difficulties in communication may make it difficult for them to remind others of this. It is important to check whether there is any evidence for such a generalised depressed state which might be influencing the occurrence of a specific problem behaviour.

Apart from atmosphere and state factors there are other kinds of general setting conditions which can predispose people towards acting inappropriately. It is a common observation, for example, that behaviour problems can be more likely to occur when the individual is not actively engaged in some kind of task. Of course not everybody can be fully occupied all of the time, but people with serious learning and behavioural problems often spend a large amount of time doing nothing or waiting for things to happen: waiting to be changed, waiting for meals, waiting for everyone to finish their meals, waiting for buses. More immediate settings which may influence behaviour are places, people, times or the amount of structure present in a situation.

Triggers and problem behaviours

If problem behaviours are learned through achieving important results for the person, then the stimuli that were present in the environment during learning will signal when such results can be achieved. By association these stimuli may come to trigger the problem behaviour. Many kinds of stimuli or events can come to act as triggers. One common trigger, for example, is individual *people*. If one person always reacts to screaming by stroking and cuddling the student (and this is something that the student likes) but other people ignore the screaming, then the presence of that particular person will come to trigger screaming, which will not occur when that person is not around. Quite often aggressive behaviour is targeted on specific 'victims'. This may be because they do not retaliate (punish the aggressor) or because they react in a way that the student finds interesting (for example, running away, crying). Over time, the presence of these 'victims' will come to trigger the aggressive behaviour of the student.

Demands are another common social trigger. Some students learn that if they respond to demands, such as requests to complete a task, with a problem behaviour (for example, banging their head, lashing out, vomiting), then the demands are removed, thus providing escape from a situation which they dislike. In this way making demands comes to trigger the problem behaviour. Unexpected changes can also act like a demand. Some people who have serious learning disabilities find the world a puzzling and unpredictable place and become very attached to routines as a means of making the world more understandable. They have difficulty predicting when changes will occur or coping with them when they take place. They may then react very badly when such changes happen (for example, a change of activity or the entry of someone into a room) and find that their reaction leads to the situation being kept the same.

There are many other ways in which specific triggers can be built up. Particular *sights* and *sounds* may act in this way. If a student loves the sight and/or sounds of scattering materials, then the presence of glass, crockery or the Lego tray can come to trigger throwing and tipping. If the student likes the sparkle of a light on

21

liquid, then the sun coming out can trigger spitting and playing with saliva. Some students have very strong irrational fears of colours or sounds (for example, the sound of an ice-cream van chimes). For reasons that are not always well understood they may be very frightened by these things and show very difficult behaviour when they see or hear them. They may then find that when they behave in this way the stimuli are removed. In this way an uncontrolled fear response becomes learned as a means of getting rid of the unwanted stimulus.

Many problem behaviours will therefore have identifiable triggers. They will occur selectively in the presence of these triggers, but not in their absence.

Results and problem behaviours

Problem behaviours may achieve a range of important results for the individual. These may be social — especially attention or escape from demands. They may be sensory: the flicker of light on saliva, the noise from head banging on a reverberating surface, the sound of breaking glass, the crying of someone whose hair has been pulled, the sight, feel and smell of faeces when smeared. They may even be straightforwardly material: there is nothing like a screaming tantrum in the back of the car for producing a bag of sweets! It is important to remember that a behaviour can be kept going even if it does not achieve its desired result every time. The reason why people keep playing fruit machines (or gamble in general) is because pay-off occurs intermittently, usually on a rather unpredictable basis. Thus a problem behaviour only needs to achieve its favoured results every so often in order for it to persist.

Assessing skills

A second major function of assessment is to generate ideas about how identified areas of need might be met. Ideas about the means of helping a person meet his needs are obtained from an assessment of his achievements and of the factors that have contributed to these achievements. Knowing a person's skills will help generate realistic ideas about the kinds of things to teach or encourage in order to help the individual meet his needs, since the most effective approach is likely to be one that builds on existing skills — skills that the individual rarely uses or skills that are already partly learned. These are called emergent skills. Thus, if one of a number of alternative skills can be taught as a means of gaining attention (for example, tapping someone on the arm, beckoning or vocalising), selection should, as far as possible, be guided by the skills that the individual already has. So, if the individual does not vocalise or sign but will look towards a person if he wants something and will occasionally approach others for attention, then teaching him to tap people on the arm to gain their attention may be the most appropriate skill to teach.

A comprehensive assessment of a person's skills is thus an essential component of the initial planning process. Assessing skills serves another very important function. Too often people are 'labelled' only in terms of their problems. Thus a person who bangs his head against solid objects in a way that causes cuts and bruises becomes known as a 'self-injurer'. In fact, he may spend very little time banging his head but it tends to be very noticeable when it occurs. Drawing attention to only this very limited aspect of the individual through the use of such a label prevents people seeing the whole person. A thorough assessment should therefore establish the individual as an achieving person, not just as somebody who has a problem.

As important as the achievements themselves are the means by which they have been achieved, since it is these methods that are likely to be most effective in teaching new skills or encouraging rarely used skills in a programme of intervention. Thus it will be important to note the conditions under which new learning is most likely to occur. These include people to whom the student is most responsive, times when he is most receptive to new information, and places were learning occurs most easily. They may also include conditions such as the best ways of presenting instructions or of holding the student's attention.

Assessing motivators

One of the most important factors that relate to learning is those things that motivate the person to perform appropriate skills. *Motivators* are the results that a person works to achieve by his actions. Every individual varies to some extent in the things that encourage or discourage his actions. On the whole, the results that people will work to achieve or avoid fall into a number of broad categories. There are *social* results, such as praise, physical closeness, smiles, eye contact, criticism or frowns, which are the response of other people to an action. There are *sensory* results, which are events that stimulate the sensory systems. Particular sights, sounds, touches and smells may be powerful motivators for some individuals. Some people, for example, like shiny or spinning objects; some dislike certain colours or sounds. Many toys are designed to provide exciting sensory consequences for playing with them (squeakers, musical toys, humming tops, 'surprise' toys). There are a number of sensory results that have a social element: stroking, tickling, massaging, being spun round, being thrown up and down, being held. For some it is important that such things be provided by a person, whereas others are more interested in the experience and do not mind whether it is provided by a person or a piece of equipment. There are *material* results. These include results such as food and drink, which affect basic life-support biological systems, or results such as favourite activities or treats. Finally, there is an important category of results which are called *symbolic* reinforcers. Symbolic reinforcers are ones which, in and of themselves, have no value. They become valued because they 'buy' access to goods and services. The most common example of a symbolic reinforcer is money. Stars or tokens can, in many ways, act like money because they can be exchanged for other important things.

Defining needs

Having carried out a full and comprehensive assessment, it should then be possible to prioritise needs which are considered to be important for the overall management of the problem behaviour. Priority areas of need should include:

(1) Reducing or eliminating the problem behaviour.
(2) Developing skills that are of direct relevance to the long-term resolution of the problem behaviour. These may be new skills which the individual has not yet learned, or they may be skills which the person has but does not use appropriately or sufficiently.

Important skills to develop are ones that are *functionally equivalent*, that is, skills that the person can use to achieve the same results as are achieved by the problem behaviour. For example, if a person spends much of the day engaging in repetitive behaviours and these behaviours are thought to provide a major source of

24

occupation and sensory stimulation for the individual, then one priority area of work is likely to be the teaching or encouraging of other means of self-occupation and other ways of achieving sensory stimulation that are more acceptable. If a person is destructive to property whenever demands are put on him, then a priority area of work may be to teach or encourage alternative ways of communicating that the demands are too difficult or ways of asking for help.

Alternatively, skills that are *physically incompatible* with the problem behaviour may be usefully developed. Physically incompatible skills are those that cannot be performed at the same time as the problem behaviour. Teaching or encouraging such skills can be a powerful way of influencing whether difficult behaviours occur. For example, a person cannot wander around a room pulling things off the shelves if he is sitting at a table painting. A person cannot engage in hand flapping while he is taking a drink to his mouth or doing other constructive activities with his hands. Sometimes it may be possible to find a skill which is both functionally equivalent and physically incompatible. For example, if holding down a pressure pad on a computer keyboard is necessary for visual stimulation to appear on a screen, this may be a powerful way of dealing with eye poking for visual stimulation.

The first major task in problem behaviour management is to define priority areas of need which are relevant to the management of problem behaviour and to establish strengths which a person has and which can be utilised to meet the needs that have been identified, as this will accelerate and facilitate change. Such a task cannot be done without a comprehensive assessment of the problem behaviour, a person's skills and the motivators which he will consistently work to achieve. In the first part of this section, the principles involved in defining priority needs and assessing strengths have been outlined. In the second part, the specific steps that must be taken to achieve this will be detailed.

B. PROCEDURES FOR FORMULATING A MANAGEMENT PLAN

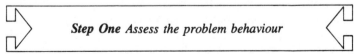

Step One Assess the problem behaviour

The first step in formulating a plan for managing a problem behaviour is to carry out a full analysis of the problem behaviour itself: to discover the situations in which it occurs (settings), the factors which set it off (triggers) and the results it achieves for the individual.

Methods of assessment

There are, essentially, three methods of carrying out such an analysis:

Interview

This is the most informal method of gathering information. Some information can usefully be obtained this way, particularly information about background factors which might be influencing the individual's behaviour (for example, major upheavals at home) but which may not be readily apparent to others. On the whole, however, whilst a general picture might be obtained using an interview method, such retrospective information, based on memory and often inadequate observations, is likely to provide an incomplete or inaccurate picture.

When collecting information using interview methods, care should be taken not to ask questions in a way which suggests that the questioner has a clear expectancy about the answer, since people often feel obliged to give answers which they think people expect them to give. This is particularly so for questions that require a Yes/No answer ('Does he . . .?'). When interviewing people about the situations that give rise to problem behaviours, it is therefore best to ask questions in a more open manner ('Tell me about . . .'). To ensure that information is as accurate as possible it is important that people interviewed have known the individual for some time and have had the opportunity to observe him in a range of situations. Questions should focus on what they have actually observed — actions, settings, triggers and results — and not on what they have heard from others or on their subjective impression.

Observation

A large amount of useful information can be obtained through systematic observation and immediate recording of details about settings, triggers and results each time a predefined behaviour occurs. A recording form, as shown in Figure 2.2, can greatly facilitate this method of data collection. The person's name should be clearly written at the top of the recording sheet, together with details of the behaviour which is to be observed. It is important that

Figure 2.2: A STAR Recording Form

Name	ANNIE			

Behaviour to be Observed	DISRUPTIVE MEALTIME BEHAVIOUR, INCLUDING TIPPING FOOD, THROWING CUTLERY.			
Date	**Setting**	**Trigger**	**Action**	**Result**
OCTOBER 10TH	DINING ROOM, LUNCHTIME, SITTING WITH TOM, PAT AND DEN.	TOM CHATTING TO PAT	ANNIE PUSHES PAT'S PLATE ACROSS THE TABLE.	TOM HAD A GO AT HER AND STOPPED TALKING TO PAT.
OCTOBER 14TH	DINING ROOM, BREAKFAST TIME, SITTING ALONE.	CALLED TO TOM WHO WAS SEEING TO SOMEONE ELSE. TOM SAID "WAIT A MINUTE."	THREW SPOON ONTO FLOOR – IGNORED – SO THREW PLATE ONTO FLOOR.	TOM SHOUTED AT HER AND MADE HER CLEAR IT UP.
OCTOBER 14TH	LUNCHTIME, DINING ROOM, SITTING AT TABLE WITH MEG, TOM, DEN & CHRIS EVERYONE TALKING.	ASKED FOR SALT. MEG PASSED IT OVER.	PUT SALT INTO MEG'S AND DEN'S FOOD.	THEY ALL TOLD HER NOT TO BE SILLY AND TO TAKE CARE OF HER OWN PLATE.

each observation be dated. Each time the behaviour occurs, the setting in which it occurs should be described (this may include the place, time of day, people present, activity, etc.); the trigger (the event immediately preceding the behaviour) should be noted; the action should be described in detail (including the length of time for which it continued, the number of times it occurred, its severity, etc.); and, finally, the result (the event which immediately followed the behaviour) should be written down. This type of recording form should be readily available and, if necessary, should travel around with the person so that recording can be done as soon as the behaviour occurs. If the behaviour is clearly defined at the top of the record sheet, then anyone coming into regular contact with the individual can help collect data. Usually at least two or three weeks of data will be needed to obtain a clear picture of the relevant factors.

Figure 2.2 illustrated how details of a particular behaviour can be recorded. From the few recordings of the behaviour that are shown, a picture of the circumstances in which disruptive behaviours occur is already emerging. In this example it seems to happen when no one is paying the person any attention, and the result of her disruptive actions seems to be that people turn to her to give her attention, albeit to tell her off. Several more recordings would provide a clearer and more consistent picture of the circumstances in which her unacceptable behaviour occurs.

There are occasions when observation over several weeks will still not provide clear-cut information about the settings, triggers and results that are associated with the problem behaviour. In such cases a more formal method such as testing may need to be used.

Testing

It is sometimes possible to assess the factors that influence a behaviour by direct testing. This is only possible, however, for behaviours that occur frequently. For example, if, after observation of a behaviour, it is unclear which specific triggers are associated with the problem behaviour, a person might be put in a number of situations where a range of triggers are presented while a measure is taken of the occurrence of the problem behaviour in each situation. Such situations might include:

(1) a high level of demand — the person being required to perform a number of tasks;
(2) a low level of demand — the person being left alone with a few activities;

(3) a high level of attention — the person being talked to and/or physically interacted with;
(4) no attention — the person being ignored and attention being given to other people.

Each situation would be presented several times over a number of days to see whether it led to a consistent change in the occurrence of the behaviour.

Interpreting assessment information

All the information collected needs to be carefully inspected. A count of the various settings, triggers and results noted in recordings made over a few weeks may show that just one or a few environmental events are consistently associated with the problem behaviour. A look at the interrelationship between them may reveal some consistent patterns. For example, the setting in which a person becomes disruptive may be one where there is a high noise level, and this may occur irrespective of the demands that may be placed on him. On the other hand, it may be that the behaviour (for example, throwing objects) occurs in specific settings (the supermarket) and only when there are specific triggers (mother stopping to chat to a friend). Recordings may reveal that the same result is consistently achieved by a behaviour (for example, getting out of unpleasant situations). Or it may become clear that a single behaviour serves a number of functions for the individual and achieves a variety of results.

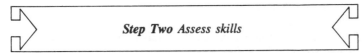

Step Two Assess skills

Having carried out an analysis of the problem behaviour, the next step is to assess the skills that a person has. Although a general overview of a person's skills is important, particular attention should be paid to those skills which do or might with encouragement serve the same function for the individual as the problem behaviour by achieving similar results. Attention should also be paid to skills that are incompatible with the problem behaviour, that is, skills it would be difficult for a person to perform at the same time as performing the unacceptable action. These skills will vary for each individual. Different environments will have different expectations (the demands in a school setting will be different from those in a family home setting,

29

for example). There is therefore no strict rule about which skills to assess. Most assessments, however, are likely to cover similar general areas: abilities to communicate and understand, abilities to get on with people, abilities to occupy one's time and to solve problems, and abilities to manage basic self-help functions such as toileting, washing, feeding and dressing.

Aims of assessment

A useful assessment is one that can aid in the planning of a teaching programme. It should therefore aim to answer the following questions:

(1) Does the individual have the skill and use it when appropriate without help or prompting? If not,
(2) Does the individual have parts of the skill but not the whole skill?
(3) Does the individual show the skill if given help?
(4) Does the individual show the skill sometimes, but not reliably or all the time?

Such a graded form of assessment provides more information than a Yes/No type of assessment, but is clearly more complicated and time consuming to carry out.

Method of assessment

As with problem behaviours, there are three ways in which skills can be assessed.

Interview

The most informal method of assessing a person's skills is to ask somebody who knows the person well As with all assessments carried out using this method, care must be taken to ask only those people who will definitely have had the opportunity to observe the person in relevant situations. Care must also be taken to ask questions in a way which does not suggest that the interviewer has any expectation about what the answer should be — as people may feel obliged to give the answer they think others want to hear. The interview should focus on what the people have themselves observed, rather than on what they have heard from others or what they think a person can do.

Observation

Whenever possible, assessment should be based on observations in the person's natural environment. Thus, to find out the skills a person has in feeding himself, it is best to observe the person during natural mealtimes. To find out the skills a person has in occupying himself, it is best to observe him during 'free' time.

Testing

Although observation can provide a lot of information, some of it may be difficult to interpret. Some skills may be difficult to assess: they may be demonstrated only rarely or there may be no opportunity to demonstrate them. For example, it may be difficult to judge a person's cooking skills if he is not allowed into the kitchen. It may take a long time to observe if a person can sign his name if this activity only has to be done once a week at the post office. In these cases it is reasonable to 'test out' the person's skills by setting up as natural a situation as possible and observing the individual's response. So one could get a form from the post office and ask the person to show how he signs his name.

Using assessment schedules to aid in the assessment of skills

An assessment of skills is made easier by having a prepared assessment schedule from which to work. Many people or institutions design their own schedules but a large number of such devices are commercially available. Details of some of these are provided in Appendix III. Some are suited to more able people, others to people who have a very profound degree of disability. Commercially available assessment tools generally take the form of checklists. Skills are grouped under major headings such as communication, socialisation, social independence, motor and leisure. Under each heading are listed a large number of individual skills, usually in an order which goes from easy to hard, those learned early in life to those learned later. Some commercially available assessment schedules will have a method of scoring whether skills are present, how much of a skill a person can perform independently and how much help he needs to perform other parts of the skill. These are the most useful assessment schedules to use. On the whole, such schedules

31

can save a lot of time, although they may need adapting for the individual. If using assessment schedules it should be remembered that they should never be taken as a rigid formula but simply as a guideline to possible skills which might be assessed.

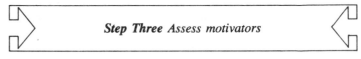

Step Three *Assess motivators*

Methods of assessment

The methods for assessing motivators are essentially the same as for skills and problem behaviours.

Interview

Important information can be obtained by asking the people who know the individual well, or even asking the person himself. When interviewing other people about an individual's preferences, it is important to focus the interview around what they have themselves observed and not around what they have heard from others or what they think the individual may like or dislike.

Observation

Observation of a person in his natural environment can provide a lot of information about the things that encourage or discourage his actions. Things that are likely to prove useful for encouraging new skills or building up existing ones are things that the person spends a lot of time with given the opportunity, and things that a person works hard to achieve. Things that are likely to be useful for discouraging inappropriate action are things that a person works hard to avoid. Emotional responses, such as laughing or crying, do not always provide reliable evidence that a thing or activity is likely to encourage or discourage behaviour. Anxiety and excitement may look very similar, and even when they are interpreted correctly their exact significance may be uncertain. For example, people will often do things they find frightening ('thrills') and may repeat actions that get them into trouble, since 'trouble' can often mean a lot of attention even though it may make them cry. The most reliable information obtained by observation is obtained from the length of time people spend on various activities and how hard they work to achieve or avoid activities and other events.

Testing

Although observation can provide a lot of information, some of it can be difficult to interpret. Some events may be very rare or may not be available at all. It is therefore possible to test out an individual's preferences in relation to positive motivators, particularly sensory or material ones. This can be done by offering the individual choices of items which it is thought they will like and recording which ones are consistently preferred. Thus a person may be offered a range of drinks, foodstuffs or sensory toys and equipment (perhaps two or three at a time) and a record is made of the item selected. By repeating the procedure several times, it is possible to see if the individual shows a clear preference for one or more items. Any such 'preferred' items may subsequently be useful as a source of positive incentive.

There is no similar test procedure for things that discourage the person. Although in theory it would be possible to construct such a test, in practice it would not be ethically acceptable to inflict a range of potentially negative events on a person. Nor is it really necessary. Such information as is needed can be gained from other sources (observation, interview).

 Step Four *Summarise assessment information*

The assessment of skills and motivators and of the problem behaviour will have produced a large amount of information. In the course of carrying out these assessments other information will have been learned more informally about the individual, which may be useful in the overall management of the problem behaviour. All this information now needs to be summarised and a general plan formulated which will be the basis of a comprehensive programme for managing the problem behaviour. Assessment information can best be summarised under two headings: *strengths* and *needs*.

Summarising strengths

A person's strengths include his skills and those important aspects of the environment which can be utilised to effect behaviour change, to help teach new skills, to build up existing skills and to reduce unacceptable behaviours. A list of a person's strengths should include information about the following STAR factors:

Settings

Settings that need to be listed are those situations that are likely to form the optimal context in which learning can take place. The most important settings factors are:

People. These may include particular people who are especially fond of the person, people to whom the person responds more positively and listens to more readily, and people in whose presence the problem behaviour rarely occurs.

Places. These may include particular places where behaviour problems are less likely to occur (for example, a structured situation such as work at school) and where new learning is more likely to occur (for example, a place where there are few distractions, such as a particular corner of a room).

Times. These include particular times of the day/week when the person is more relaxed, when problem behaviours are least likely to occur and when learning is most likely to take place. (One person may, for example, be most relaxed after a bath in the evening and engage in less self-stimulatory behaviour then than at other times of the day; another may co-operate better with learning early in the day.)

Triggers

It is important to list the things that regularly 'set off' important actions. For example, there may be optimal ways of triggering desirable behaviours in an individual (perhaps by showing him what to do, or by physically guiding him through an activity, or by giving only simple instructions). There may be effective ways of gaining a person's attention so that he can attend to teaching tasks, or of stopping inappropriate activities (for example, calling the student's name loudly). These are important triggers to note.

Actions

These are skills that a person already has which might be encouraged or built up in some way in order to replace the problem behaviour. They are also skills that can be used as a starting point for teaching other new skills. For example, if a person can knit, likes listening to music and can operate a tape recorder, then these could be the starting point for teaching him to occupy himself in his spare time. In a sense, therefore, all of a person's skills need to be listed. The more skills a person has, the more general the list is likely to be. For example, if a person has good language skills, it may be sufficient to summarise these with a statement such as 'Can communicate his needs and feelings and relate experiences', whereas, for a person who has only limited communication skills, it may be necessary to itemise each individual skill (for example, 'Can indicate if he wants to go to the toilet, will sign "drink" and "please", will take person to what he wants if can't reach it himself').

Results

Important strengths to list are the things that serve as motivators and that encourage the person to use his skills and behave appropriately. They include the things the person likes (social, sensory and material reinforcers) and activities he enjoys doing. Other important results to summarise are ones that actively discourage a person from performing inappropriate activities (for example, forfeiting an outing if an aggressive outburst occurs).

Summarising needs

Alongside the summary of strengths it is important to summarise priority ares of work which must be undertaken with the individual in order to help resolve the problem behaviour. They are best summarised as a list of 'needs'. Needs are statements about skills the person needs to learn or extend, behaviours that need to be reduced, and experiences that a person may need to have. The list of needs will subsequently be used to establish teaching objectives and management plans. It is important to note that statements about a person's needs are not statements about the person's weaknesses. A summary of weaknesses is not useful for establishing teaching objectives and management plans: it merely promotes negative thinking, which cannot serve any benefit for the individual.

In relation to the management of a problem behaviour, a needs list should include statements about the following:

(1) Behaviours which need to be reduced or eliminated.
(2) New skills that need to be learned which will reduce the likelihood of the problem behaviour occurring. (These are likely to be functionally equivalent or physically incompatible skills.)
(3) Existing skills that occur infrequently, but if strengthened would decrease the likelihood of the problem behaviour occurring.
(4) Aspects of the environment (setting or triggers) that may need to be altered in order to decrease the likelihood of the problem behaviour occurring.

Writing a strengths and needs list

A strengths and needs list can be written on a recording sheet like the one shown in Figure 2.3. The following points should be noted about the strengths and needs list illustrated there:

(1) It contains many more strengths than needs.
(2) Strengths include information about settings, triggers and results which might be relevant to a teaching programme, in addition to information about the person's important skills.
(3) The needs list includes statements about behaviours that need to be decreased, alternative behaviours that need to be learned in order to replace the inappropriate behaviour, and existing skills that need to be built up in order to minimise the opportunity for practising the inappropriate behaviours.
(4) Needs are positively stated.

A strengths and needs list is best compiled by all those who will be involved in drawing up and implementing programmes of change, since it forms the basis of the overall management strategy that will be adopted to help the person overcome his problem behaviours.

SUMMARY

When a person who has severe learning disabilities is identified as having a serious behaviour problem that requires intervention, a considerable amount of preparatory work needs to be completed before a useful programme can be started. Hasty decisions based on inadequate information and prompted by a feeling of urgency will fail in the long term. A long-term perspective is essential, not least because problem behaviours are likely to serve important functions in the life of the individual concerned. Thus, if problem behaviours are to be eliminated, then other skills must be encouraged and new skills developed to replace those unwanted actions. This requires a period of assessment of the problem behaviour, of the person's skills and of the factors which might promote new learning and encourage behaviour change. From such an assessment, priority needs can be established, which will form the basis of a comprehensive management strategy.

Figure 2.3: A strengths and needs list

Name PETER (8 YEARS)	**Date** MARCH 3RD
Strengths	**Needs**

Strengths	Needs
(ACTIONS) FULLY MOBILE HAS A NICE SMILE CAN CONCENTRATE FOR UP TO 10 MINUTES WILL FIND HIMSELF ACTIVITIES TO OCCUPY HIMSELF SINGS WELL HAS A LOT OF SPEECH (USES 1 OR 2 WORD PHRASES) IS DRY DURING THE DAY COMMUNICATES MOST OF HIS NEEDS, VERBALLY AND BY GESTURE. CAN PUT ON HIS COAT & TROUSERS WHEN SUPERVISED WILL TIDY UP HIS TOYS & REMEMBER WHERE THEY GO (SETTINGS) BEHAVES NICELY WHEN ON HIS BICYCLE IS BETTER WHEN HE CAN CHOOSE WHAT TO DO WORKS BETTER IN A QUIET STRUCTURED SITUATION (TRIGGERS) WILL LISTEN TO INSTRUCTIONS WHEN TOLD "PUT YOUR HANDS ON YOUR LAP" RESPONDS TO INSTRUCTIONS OF UP TO 2 WORDS (RESULTS) LIKES OUTDOOR ACTIVITIES. ESPECIALLY SLIDES AND GOING TO THE PARK. LIKES TOYS WITH WHEELS LIKES LEGO LOVES FOOD. ESPECIALLY CHOCOLATE LIKES TO RIDE IN THE CAR WITH HIS DAD LIKES SAND AND WATER	TO STOP THROWING OBJECTS AT PEOPLE TO CALM HIMSELF MORE QUICKLY WHEN AGITATED TO STAY AWAY FROM DANGEROUS ACTIVITIES TO INDICATE APPROPRIATELY IF HE DOES NOT WANT TO DO SOMETHING. TO SPEND MORE TIME DOING CONSTRUCTIVE ACTIVITIES. TO HAVE THE ORDER OF ACTIVITIES EXPLAINED TO HIM BEFORE BEING EXPECTED TO DO THEM.

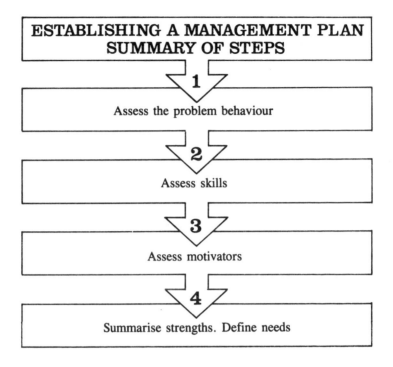

3

DEFINING GOALS

The approach to behaviour change presented in this book stresses the need for efficiency. People who have learning disabilities cannot afford inefficiency from their teachers, as this will slow down their progress. One aspect of efficiency is precision: in particular, knowing *exactly* what a programme of change is to achieve. A summary of a person's needs will provide fairly general statements about areas that need to be worked on (for example, communication

Figure 3.1

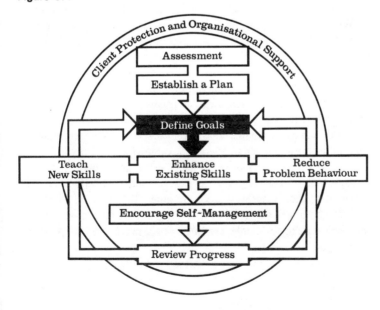

or self-occupation). It does not provide specific goals. 'Needs' must, therefore, be translated into specific goals.

For people with serious learning difficulties a very efficient method of achieving change has been shown to be one based on a graded and systematic approach. This requires a careful analysis of the tasks involved and a plan for achieving change in each identified area of need using a step-by-step approach.

A. GENERAL PRINCIPLES FOR GOAL SETTING

Long-term goals

In the first place 'needs' must be translated into long-term goals for change. Such goals must be precise and specific. They must be expressed in terms of observable and specific behaviour, not 'inner states' or abstract generalisations. To give an example, the goal of teaching an individual to be more 'sociable' is a general statement about an abstract notion of 'sociability'. It can be interpreted in a number of ways. It therefore provides no clear goals for teaching. Furthermore, it does not allow an assessment of whether the goal has been achieved. A more precise goal is one which refers to a specific behaviour, for example, 'initiating conversation at the dinner table' or 'playing football with other children in the playground'. Only by being precise and specific about goals of change is it possible for people to know exactly what they are striving to achieve, how they should proceed and whether or not they have achieved their goals.

It is to be expected that these goals may take time to achieve. Nevertheless, it would be unwise to set long-term goals which the individual would be unable to achieve within, say, 6 to 9 months. It would be better to set smaller achievable goals and review these at the end of this period rather than leave goals unchanged for perhaps 1 or 2 years. Long-term goals would be likely to be forgotten over such lengthy periods of time. This is particularly so when teaching new skills, since it is likely to take far longer to teach new skills than to strengthen existing ones or even to reduce problem behaviours.

Breaking complex tasks into steps

Long-term goals are likely to involve a complex task — too complex for a person with learning difficulties to master in one go. Therefore, in order to make it easier for the student to learn, the task needs to be broken down into small steps which can be taught one at a time. Many complex skills are taught in this manner. Driving a car, for example, involves a number of skills such as steering, clutch control, reversing, and using the highway code. These many skills, which combine to form the very complex task of driving, are rarely taught to new drivers during their first lesson but are broken down into a series of steps which are taught over a number of lessons. As each step is mastered, another is introduced.

People with serious learning difficulties can find apparently simple skills complex. For them, even simple skills may need to be broken down into steps and taught one step at a time, in a graded way. By breaking tasks down it can quickly become apparent just how complex even the simplest of skills really are. For example, the skill of drinking a cup of coffee requires the ability to look at the cup, reach the arm towards it, grasp and lift it to the mouth with one hand without spilling. Brushing one's hair requires the ability to hold the brush at the correct angle to the head, pull the brush through the hair in downward strokes, pull the brush out of the hair after each stroke, deal systematically with knots, and work evenly round the head so that all the hair is brushed. It is little wonder that children can take years to master the skill.

Breaking a task into steps or component skills enables teachers to assess more accurately how much of the task the individual can already perform and which aspects he still needs to learn. It also allows a skill to be taught systematically in a step-by-step manner.

Organising steps for teaching

There are a number of ways in which steps can be organised for skill teaching and problem behaviour management.

Part-task chaining. This method involves teaching the steps in a task one at a time. Face washing, for example, might be taught by putting the soap on the student's face and getting him to rinse off the soap. A student might be taught to operate a video recorder by getting him to select the VTR channel on the TV and then doing the rest of the steps for the student. As each step is mastered, a new one is added (putting soap on the face, loading the tape, in the example above). Thus the steps in the task are seen as links in a chain. As one link is mastered another is added on until the chain (skill) is complete. There are two ways in which the steps in a task can be linked in teaching: forward chaining and backward chaining.

Forward chaining. This involves teaching the skill, starting with the first step in the sequence while the teacher completes or helps the individual to complete the remainder of the sequence. Once the first step is mastered, the second step is added to the first and the two steps are taught together, with the teacher completing or helping the individual through the remaining steps. Then the third step is added, and so on until the final step is reached. A skill such as pointing, for example, might be taught using a forward chaining sequence: a person being taught first to stretch out the arm, then to shape his hand correctly and finally to line up the outstretched arm with the object, hand shaped correctly in a pointing position.

Backward chaining. This involves teaching the last step in the sequence first. Once this step is mastered, the penultimate step is linked with the final step, and so on, until all steps have been learned. A skill such as eating with a spoon might be taught using a backward chaining procedure: a person being taught to move the spoon to the mouth when the spoon is held by the teacher until about 3 cm from the mouth, then 9 cm from the mouth, and so on until he is able to lift the loaded spoon unaided from the plate to the mouth. A skill such as buttoning a coat might also be taught using a backward chaining procedure, with the teacher pushing the button half-way through the buttonhole and the person pulling it through the rest of the way, then the teacher pushing the button only a quarter way through the buttonhole, and the person pulling it through the rest of the way, then the teacher lining up the button with the buttonhole and the person pushing the button into the buttonhole and pulling it out the other side and so on, until the person is able to line up all the buttons on the coat and do them up independently.

Whole-task teaching. This approach takes the student through the whole skill every time it is practised. As much (or as little) help as is needed is given at every stage to ensure completion. Thus, in the examples given earlier, the student would participate actively in all aspects of washing and of using the video recorder. Progress would be effected through a gradual reduction in the amount of help given at all stages in the task (see Section Four).

Shaping. Shaping is a method of building up a skill by reinforcing behaviours shown by the student that are closest to the desired objective. As these are built up, the basis of reinforcement is shifted to a behaviour which is even more like the desired objective. Thus, little by little the student learns to behave more and more like the desired objective. For example, a person may never sit next to others in group activities and resist any physical guidance to trigger this behaviour. He may, however, often sit on a chair about 10 feet from the group. A powerful reinforcer (see Section Four) could be given each time the student remained seated for a predetermined time (for example, 1 minute) at a distance of 10 feet from the group. Once this was happening, the chair could be move a little closer and reinforcement delivered for sitting 9 feet from the group for a given period of time. This process could be continued until the student was sitting in the group. Reinforcement could then be shifted in a similar way to help the student sit for longer periods (for example, 1 minute, 3 minutes and then 5 minutes).

Setting short-term objectives

Teaching skills step by step reduces the risk of failure and increases the chance of success. Working to reduce behaviour problems in stages also increases the chance of achieving and seeing progress. By succeeding, a person is more likely to remain interested in the learning situation, and the teacher, too, is rewarded by seeing achievements rather than no progress. Setting shorter terms goals and objectives can therefore be an important source of motivation for both student and teacher. It provides a more continuous sense of achievement and encourages the persistence so essential to overcoming serious behaviour difficulties. The final step in a comprehensive teaching plan, therefore, is to set clear and precise short-term objectives based on a breakdown of the task being taught and a decision on how best to present the task to the student. Such objectives should be achievable within a short space of time, perhaps 3 to 4 weeks.

There is an additional reason for breaking long-term goals into a series of short-term objectives. It is most unlikely that the 'right' approach to achieving the long-term goal will be found straight away. In setting short-term objectives one is providing the

43

opportunity not just to review achievements regularly but, in the light of this, to review the means being used to reach objectives. This allows programmes to be modified and adjusted regularly in line with progress made.

There are a number of steps which need to be taken after a management plan has been drawn up. 'Needs' which have been identified must now be translated into long-term goals. Then, having analysed the tasks involved and broken them down into a series of small steps, these should be translated into very precise short-term objectives for change which will be the immediate focus of programmes of change. In the first part of this section the principles involved in establishing specific short-term goals have been outlined. In the second part, the steps that need to be followed to establish such specific and immediate goals are detailed.

B. PROCEDURES FOR ESTABLISHING SPECIFIC GOALS

Having listed a person's strengths and identified priority areas of work in the form of 'needs', the next stage is to decide how these needs can be met and to set specific goals in areas of skill building and problem-behaviour reduction to meet these needs.

 Step One *Translate needs into long-term goals*

Selecting long-term goals

There are usually a number of possible ways of meeting a person's identified needs. For example, the expressed need 'To use appropriate means of letting people know what he wants' could be met in a variety of ways, such as teaching the student the names of objects, teaching the signs for specific objects, teaching a more general sign for 'please' or, alternatively, simply teaching the student to take people over to what he wants. If long-term goals are to have an impact on the problem behaviour, they need to be achieved as quickly as possible. The best way, therefore, to select such goals is to look at the skills which the person already has (these should be summarised in the strengths list) and, if possible, to encourage their increased usage; alternatively, use these as a foundation for new skills. Using the example above, if the person uses a lot of gestures but does not vocalise, then it would be more appropriate to aim to teach a range of signs rather than try to teach the names of objects.

Writing long-term goals

Long-term goals should describe in specific terms what the person will be doing after the programmes of change using words that refer as much as possible to easily observed behaviours, rather than unobservable 'inner states' or dispositions. Table 3.1 lists several examples of long-term goals which are expressed in words which relate to observable behaviours. For comparison, words which refer to less observable states (referred to as nebulous notions) have also been listed. Whilst it would be easy to know whether or not the behaviours which can be seen are occurring, it would be difficult to judge when the 'nebulous notions' were achieved. Such lack of clarity in a long-term goals would be likely to create disagreements among people, which in turn would hinder the development of effective programmes of change.

Long-term goals need to be written using words that refer to actions that can be readily observed. They may be observed as present or absent according to whether a behaviour is to be increased

Table 3.1: Examples of long-term goals relating to observable behaviours vs. less observable states

Nebulous notions	Things we can see
Develop grammar	Name objects in picture books
Improve social relationships	Roll a ball back and forth with another child
Listen to stories	Sit down during story time
Be more co-operative	Wash dishes after lunch
Improve emotional adjustment	Lie down screaming less than three times a week
Improve concentration span	Complete plug assembly without leaving work station
Improve sexual adjustment	Masturbate only in own room or toilet cubicle
Develop potential	Master five new skills on community living checklist
Be happier	Smile back when smiled at
Learn colours	Name colours red, blue, green
Understand the concept '3'	Put 3 packets of cereal and 3 tins of beans into shopping trolley

or decreased. In addition, they should specify the circumstances in which actions are to occur. Circumstances, in this case, refer to settings in which the action will occur or triggers that will be used to elicit the actions (the amount of help that will be given).

Table 3.2 illustrates how needs can be translated into long-term goals. It should be noted that these goals are stated in terms of unambiguous behaviours which can be easily seen, and they specify clearly the circumstances in which the behaviours will be performed once the long-term goal is achieved.

Table 3.2: Translating needs into long-term goals

1.	*Need:*	To stop throwing objects at people
	Long-term goal:	Will not throw things at people or on to the floor (action) in the classroom (circumstances)
2.	*Need:*	To calm himself when agitated
	Long-term goal:	Will practise relaxation (action) for 10 minutes each day when told (circumstances)
3.	*Need:*	To come away from dangerous activities when told
	Long-term goal:	Will respond appropriately to the instruction 'Come here' (action) when out on walks with staff (circumstances)
4.	*Need:*	To indicate appropriately if he does not want to do something
	Long-term goal:	Will say 'No' (action) if he does not want what is offered (circumstances)
5.	*Need:*	To increase time spent on constructive activities
	Long-term goal:	Will play alone with Lego bricks (action) for 15 minutes in the evening while Mum prepares dinner (circumstances)
6.	*Need:*	To have the order of activities explained before being expected to do them
	Long-term goal:	Key worker will prepare daily pictorial timetable and show it to client (action) every morning after breakfast (circumstances)

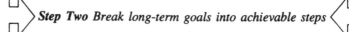

Step Two Break long-term goals into achievable steps

Long-term goals will take several months to achieve. The next step, therefore, is to break long-term goals into steps that are small enough for the student to achieve within a short space of time — no more than four weeks. To do this, the task which is the long-term goal must be analysed at two levels.

Tasks as component skills

The first thing to consider is whether the task is made up of one or several separate skills which have been combined. For example, eating with a spoon requires the following separate skills:

(a) gripping the spoon,
(b) loading the spoon,
(c) lifting the spoon to the mouth and, perhaps,
(d) chewing the food.

The task of playing Ludo requires the following separate skills:

(a) sitting in one place for at least a few minutes,
(b) looking at the die and board,
(c) counting up to six,
(d) taking turns,
(e) recognising and matching colours.

Skills as steps

Once a task has been broken down into its component skills, each component skill must be further broken down into a series of small steps which will take the individual from his present level of skill to the desired level. Thus the skill of lifting a loaded spoon to the mouth can be broken down into a number of small steps:

(1) Lifting food to mouth when spoon is 1 inch from mouth.
(2) Lifting food to mouth when spoon is 3 inches from mouth.
(3) Lifting food to mouth when spoon is 6 inches from mouth.
(4) Lifting food to mouth when spoon is loaded and left on the plate.

The component skills 'Looking at die and board' during a game of Ludo can be broken down into the following small steps:

(1) Looking at die and board briefly when it is taken out of the box.
(2) Looking at die as it is thrown.
(3) Looking at die as it is thrown until it settles on the table.
(4) Looking at die long enough for spots to be counted, and observing the counter being moved.
(5) Looking at die and board while two people have a turn at throwing the die and moving their counters.

There is no 'right' number of steps into which a task can be broken down. What is important is that the steps are small enough for the individual to master within a short space of time — no more than 3 or 4 weeks. If the steps are mastered very quickly, then subsequent steps can be made larger. If, on the other hand, the individual experiences considerable difficulty in learning a step, then it may be necessary to break that step down further to even smaller steps.

Just as there is no 'right' number of steps into which a task can be broken down, so too there is no 'right' way to perform a task. Most skills can be performed in a variety of ways. For example, a jumper may be removed by (a) crossing the arms in front of the body, gripping the sides of the jumper at the base and stretching both arms up over the head; (b) reaching one arm over the shoulder, gripping the jumper at the back of the neck and pulling it over the head; (c) gripping an armhole with one hand and pushing the other arm, elbow first, through the armhole.

Some complex skills may require a good deal of imagination on the part of the teacher to get the person from his present level of skill to the objective skill. In deciding how to teach a task and on the number of steps into which it should be broken down, it is important to consider what is realistic for the individual, to capitalise on the individual's existing skills and to tailor the teaching to the student's abilities and preferences as much as possible.

Breaking down problem behaviours

Behaviours may be identified as a problem because they occur too frequently, in too many settings, because they go on for too long, because they are too severe or because they occur at all. The long-term objective may be to eliminate the behaviour completely or to reduce it to an acceptable level. However, just as it may take several months to teach new skills so, too, it may take a long time to reduce or eliminate the problem behaviour. By setting small achievable goals, progress is more likely to be seen and people will be encouraged to persist with programme efforts. Thus a long-term objective of eliminating a frequently occurring problem behaviour may be broken down into steps which entail the behaviour occurring less and less frequently at each step, or being eliminated first in one setting (for example, morning school), then another (playground), then another (dining room) until it is eliminated in all settings.

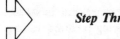

Step Three *Organise steps for teaching*

Having broken down tasks into component skills and broken down each skill and problem behaviour into a series of small, achievable steps, it is necessary then to plan the most appropriate order in which to present the steps to the student.

Whole-task teaching or part-task chaining

There are no rigid rules for selecting whole-task versus part-task procedures. If a person can perform several parts of a skill, then whole-task teaching may be more appropriate. If he is unable to perform any steps of a skill, then part-task chaining is likely to be preferred. For example, if a student can grip a spoon and move it in a controlled way, then whole-task teaching of feeding — to scoop and to lift the spoon to the mouth — may be appropriate. If, on the other hand, his skills are more limited, such that even gripping the spoon poses problems for him, then part-task teaching may be more appropriate, in order to avoid too many demands on the individual within a single teaching situation.

Backward or forward chaining

Certain skills can logically be taught in just a single sequence. For example, a child needs to be able to sit on the toilet before he can use it. In such cases, the skill itself determines the order of teaching. Other skills could be taught using either backward or forward chaining. For example, a person could be taught to tie shoe laces by being taught, first, to pick up and cross the laces over. Alternatively, he could be taught, first, to pull the bow tight, the teacher having completed the initial steps of the skill for him. On the whole, when either procedure can be used, it is considered preferable to use backward chaining. This is because, by teaching the final step first, the task is always completed by the student during learning. This can act as a source of encouragement and motivation because the objective is always achieved and because finishing a task implies succeeding.

Chaining or shaping

Chaining procedures tend to be more efficient for new skill teaching than shaping, since the teacher is able, in many respects, to set the pace for teaching and skill performance. Shaping requires waiting for the student to perform the target action of his own accord. This may occur less consistently than when chaining is used. When possible, therefore, chaining should be used. Chaining is appropriate when it is possible to provide prompts to help the student complete each step of a task (see Section Four). However, prompting can sometimes be difficult. Some actions, such as looking or vocalising, are very hard to prompt, and some students may ignore or resist prompting. In these cases, shaping may be the most appropriate procedure.

 Step Four *Set short-term behavioural objectives*

Having organised a strategy for presenting the steps that will lead to the long-term goal, the final step in planning programmes of behaviour change is to establish the immediate goal of the intervention, in other words, to specify a short-term behavioural objective.

Short-term behavioural objectives are statements about the immediate goal of any intervention programme. A student should be able to achieve such objectives in no less than a week and in no more than a month. Achievement of a series of short-term objectives will lead to the ultimate attainment of the long-term goal. It is essential that short-term objectives are stated very precisely so that there can be no doubt when they have been achieved, since achievement of a short-term objective is a prerequisite for moving on to the next objective.

Writing a short-term behavioural objective

A precise behavioural objective should state: *who* will do *what* under what *circumstances* to what *degree of success*.

Who — The name of the individual who will be performing the action in question.
Will do what — The action that the person will be observed to carry out (or not carry out in the case of a problem behaviour).
Under what circumstances — The conditions under which the action is to be performed. This includes information about the settings in which the action is to occur (if relevant) and triggers (prompts) which will be provided to enable the individual to perform the action.

50

To what degree of success — This refers to the frequency with which an action needs to be demonstrated under the given circumstances to be sure that the step has been mastered.

Examples of precisely stated short-term objectives are illustrated in Table 3.3, and an illustration of how a single long-term goal can be achieved via a series of specific short-term objectives is shown in Table 3.4. Programmes based on short-term objectives are reviewed regularly to see whether success has been achieved according to the criterion stated. If progress does not occur within a few weeks, steps can be made smaller and more limited short-term objectives set. If objectives are achieved in less than a week, then subsequent steps could be made larger and objectives altered accordingly.

Table 3.3: Examples of short-term behavioural objectives

Who	Will do what	Under what circumstances	To what degree of success
Peter	will come to his teacher	on request	3 times out of 3 during playtime, for 2 weeks
Mary	will say 'no'	if offered an activity she does not want to do	three times during morning work
John	will build with Lego bricks	alongside Mark with occasional reminders from his mum	for 15 minutes 3 times in 1 week
Maggie	will lie on the floor with her eyes closed	with reminders to stay 'calm' and 'relaxed' every 20 seconds	for 10 minutes each day for 5 consecutive days

SUMMARY

Before implementing a comprehensive behaviour management plan, such a plan must be translated into concrete goals for change. These goals must be realistic and attainable within a short period of time. This requires an analysis and breakdown of the task involved, so that short-term immediate goals can be drawn up. A lot of detailed work is required in this process. However, such work at this stage saves time in the long run as it enhances efficiency in teaching and problem behaviour management.

Table 3.4: Reaching a long-term goal by a series of short-term behavioural objectives

Long-term goal: Peter will practise relaxation for 10 minutes each day when told

Who	Will do what	Under what circumstances	To what degree of success
1. Peter	will lie on floor	with adult continually talking in soothing voice, physically prompting him to stay still	for 30 seconds, on 5 successive sessions
2. Peter	will lie on floor	with adult continually talking in soothing voice, verbally prompting him to stay still	for 30 seconds, on 5 successive sessions
3. Peter	will lie on floor, eyes closed	with verbal prompts to be 'calm' and 'relaxed', every 5 seconds	for 30 seconds, on 5 successive sessions
4. Peter	will lie on floor, eyes closed	with verbal prompts to be 'calm' and 'relaxed', every 5 seconds	for 1 minute on 5 consecutive sessions
5. Peter	will lie on floor, eyes closed	with verbal prompts to be 'calm' and 'relaxed', every 5 seconds	for 5 minutes on 5 consecutive sessions
6. Peter	will lie on floor, eyes closed	with verbal prompts to be 'calm' and 'relaxed' every 10 seconds	for 5 minutes on 5 consecutive sessions
7. Peter	will lie on floor, eyes closed	with verbal prompts to be 'calm' and 'relaxed' every 20 seconds	for 5 minutes on 5 consecutive sessions
8. Peter	will lie on floor, eyes closed	with verbal prompts to be 'calm' and 'relaxed' every 20 seconds	for 10 minutes on 5 consecutive sessions

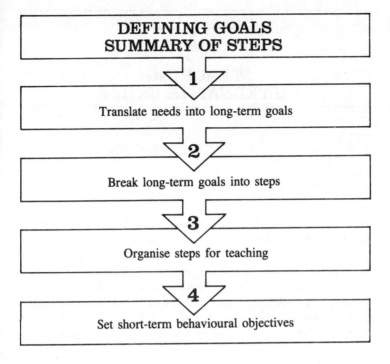

DEFINING GOALS
SUMMARY OF STEPS

1

Translate needs into long-term goals

2

Break long-term goals into steps

3

Organise steps for teaching

4

Set short-term behavioural objectives

4
TEACHING
ALTERNATIVE SKILLS

A central theme of this book is that problem behaviours are meaningful actions which serve an important function for the individual. If a long-term solution to a problem is to be achieved, the individual must be provided with appropriate alternative ways of expressing the same function and achieving the same goals. More often than not this requires teaching the individual new skills. Skills can be learned in many ways — for example, they can be learned by watching others, or they can be learned by trial and error — but people with

Figure 4.1

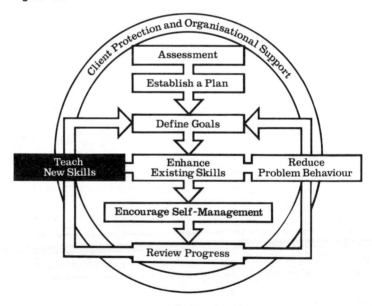

severe learning disabilities often find it difficult to make progress without active and structured help from those around them. Structured help can be provided by systematic manipulation of settings, triggers and results. This requires considerable planning on the part of the person carrying out the teaching. But such planning saves time in the long run and makes it far more likely that the individual will learn.

A. GENERAL PRINCIPLES FOR SKILL TEACHING

The approach to teaching new skills which is adopted is one that seeks to make learning as error-free as possible. Making mistakes can never be prevented altogether. However, prolonged failure can have a disastrous effect on the learner both in terms of discouragement and in terms of learning bad habits. Errors can be avoided by planning and presenting tasks in a way that maximises the probability that the learner will succeed and that minimises the probability of failure. Error-free learning is achieved by careful control over settings, triggers and results during teaching.

Settings for skill teaching

Setting factors are those general aspects of an environment or an individual that provide broad information about types of behaviour which are possible or appropriate or which predispose the person to act in a particular way. For example, the kitchen is a setting for some behaviours (such as washing up, food preparation, cooking) but not for others (for example, dressing). The state induced by extensive physical exercise may predispose the individual towards some behaviours (sitting quietly, sleeping) rather than others (such as rushing about, or engaging in heavy physical work). Feeling miserable may predispose an individual to avoid meeting others and engaging in extensive social interaction. Being in a noisy and crowded room may induce the individual to look around and attend to the commotion rather than concentrate on a difficult learning task. Setting conditions are thus an important source of influence upon behaviour and need to be taken into account when planning a teaching programme in order to create the optimal conditions for learning.

Triggers for new skills

All behaviour has some sort of trigger which sets it off in a given situation at a given time. For example, in the morning an alarm clock may be the trigger for getting out of bed, getting out of bed triggers entry to the bathroom, and the bathroom triggers toileting and washing. Completion of these activities triggers a return to the bedroom, the bedroom triggers dressing, and so on. Being asked by a shop assistant 'Can I help?' will trigger the customer to ask for what is wanted. All behaviours have some kind of trigger, and many things can act as a trigger: sights, sounds, places, people, materials, previous behaviours in a sequence and speech are just some examples. When teaching a new skill it is important to know what would be the natural triggers for the skill when it is mastered. However, these natural triggers may not exert any influence at the beginning of teaching. Thus, if a student cannot speak or understand, then a question such as 'Can I help?' triggers no particular response. In teaching new skills it may therefore not be sufficient to rely on natural triggers. It may be necessary to provide extra signals or help (arbitrary triggers) which ensure that the student actually carries out the behaviour and gets a chance to learn. Such additional triggers are called prompts. It may also be necessary to avoid introducing into the learning situation triggers that set off behaviours that interfere with learning.

Planning results for skill learning

Results are critical factors in behaviour change. In skill teaching, it is particularly important to plan results both for correct performance of a new skill and for errors. Reinforcers are the results that occur when the skill is shown correctly. 'Correct' in this context means being shown at the level appropriate for the teaching programme — if the student carries out successfully what is required. This will of course vary according to the stage of training. At the beginning of a programme, placing a piece of puzzle with physical help may be correct. At a later stage the student may need to assemble all the pieces independently in order to be correct. The amount the student has to do in order to be reinforced is part of the teaching plan. The reinforcer itself serves both to *inform* the student that what was done was correct and to *encourage* the student to keep practising.

There are many categories of reinforcer — social, sensory, material and symbolic. These were described earlier in Section Two.

In every-day life, successful use of a skill can be followed naturally by one of these categories of reinforcer. For example, the natural reinforcer for saying 'Can I have the ball, please?' is getting the ball to play with. The natural reinforcer for using food utensils is that one gets to eat. Such natural reinforcers can be the most powerful way of responding when a student is correct.

Sometimes, however, students do not find natural results immediately meaningful, either because there is a long delay between the action and the result (as between work and play, getting dressed and getting breakfast) or because the natural result is not a powerful enough source of motivation for the student to persist with learning. Thus, arbitrary reinforcers have an important role to play, particularly in the early stages of a skill teaching programme. They can be delivered immediately a skill is performed and they can increase the student's motivation to succeed. At the same time, by being paired with the natural result of performing a skill, they can increase the strength and value of the natural result. Many people with serious learning disabilities do not, for example, find social results, such as praise or attention, meaningful. By pairing these results with arbitrary results which are powerful reinforcers for the individual, such as favourite foods or activities, praise or attention can themselves acquire reinforcing properties.

It is important to note that usage of arbitrary results is quite normal practice. In early development there is often ecstatic praise (social reinforcement) for the child's first few steps or first use of the potty. Praise is not the natural reinforcer for walking or using the potty, but serves to encourage the child to keep practising until the natural reinforcers become meaningful (factors such as being able to see and reach more, move around more freely, feeling dry, and completing activities without interruption for changing).

Repeated practice

Learning requires a certain amount of repetition if a skill is to become consolidated and truly useful for the learner. Sometimes natural opportunities to learn occur only infrequently: getting dressed may occur only once a day, cookery sessions may take place only once a week. This may make it difficult for the person with learning disabilities to consolidate skills. Such consolidation seems to occur best if the learner has the opportunity for daily practice of a skill and within each daily practice can repeat the learning process several times over. Short daily 'sessions' with several 'trials per session' is a useful model for effective teaching. Some skills fit into this naturally: playing with bricks is something a child may do each day, and every time such play occurs there will be several opportunities for learning how to build them up. To fit other skills into this approach may, however, require constructing special teaching sessions in a rather arbitrary way.

Generalisation through graded change

A distinction between *natural* and *arbitrary* STAR factors is very important. In relation to skills, 'natural' refers to the settings and triggers that operate in the real world to tell the individual when a particular skill is appropriate. It refers to the results that maintain the performance of that skill in the real world. 'Arbitrary' refers to the special settings, triggers, and results that it may be necessary to introduce in teaching in order to ensure that learning occurs, but that do not occur in the normal course of events in the real world. For example, lighting the gas (to boil up a kettle for tea) is done once only, usually in a home or appropriate work setting, with appropriate materials (kettle, gas, tap, matches) triggered by feeling thirsty or a particular time of day. The result is having a cup of tea to drink. Usually, this sequence might occur only a few times per day and the pay-off for lighting the gas occurs a considerable time after the event. In order to teach gas-lighting effectively and efficiently, one tactic would be to get the individual to practise lighting (and turning off) several times over, perhaps two or three times a day. Setting and trigger factors might include the presence of an instructor, the specific instructions given, and any physical or other help required. In order to motivate practice by the learner, praise might be used for successful lighting.

This way of teaching, though effective, introduces a lot of arbitrary events (instructor, prompts, praise) which will not necessarily be present in the real world under natural circumstances. For the person who has serious learning disabilities this is likely to mean that, although learning will occur, the skill will only be used when the arbitrary factors are present and will not therefore become functional in every-day life. The learner would have difficulty in generalising from the arbitrary situation in which teaching occurred to the natural situation in which every-day practice is required. Teaching efforts are wasted if skills taught do not generalise to the student's every-day world. There is therefore a need to build bridges from arbitrary to natural events.

In order to resolve the dilemma of introducing arbitrary factors into the teaching situation, it is important to consider the idea of graded change. Graded change is an effective way of ensuring that what is learned becomes useful and generalised. It involves changing one thing at a time and changing each item in a series of small steps. Thus, following the example given earlier of teaching a student to light the gas, the instructor could gradually decrease the help given and the use of praise. Once the skill was mastered, teaching could be shifted to the places and times where the skills were required in every-day practice, and the attention of the student would gradually be drawn to the other relevant cues (own feelings of thirst, time on the clock).

The notion of graded change is present also in the idea of teaching tasks in a step-by-step manner, as described in Section Three. This enables skills to be taught in a gradual fashion using a series of specific short-term objectives. The idea of graded change is central to successful skill teaching. It is a process by which the student is 'moved on' from learning one part of a skill to another and by which he is 'moved on' from performing skills in arbitrary conditions to the situations in which the skills need to be performed in every-day life. Skill teaching requires frequently and systematically moving the student on through a series of short-term objectives towards more complete usage of a skill and from arbitrary to natural STAR factors, towards more generalised usage of a skill.

These outline the general principles involved in the STAR approach to skill teaching. Teaching skills in this way requires planning and preparation. The second part of this section details the specific steps that need to be taken to build up high-quality teaching programmes based on the principles that have been outlined.

B. DEVELOPING SKILL TEACHING PROGRAMMES

Following the assessment of a person's skills and of his problem behaviour, as outlined in Section Two, specific learning needs will have been identified for the student. From these, long-term teaching goals will have been established. These will then have been broken down into a series of short-term objectives which the student should be able to achieve within a short space of time (Section Three). The next stage is to plan teaching programmes that will ensure the achieving of these short-term objectives.

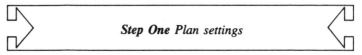

Step One Plan settings

Two important types of setting condition need to be considered when planning a teaching programme. These are settings that maximise the likelihood of learning a new skill, and settings that predispose the student towards disruptive behaviour.

Settings that maximise the likelihood of learning

These are the conditions that give the student the greatest chance of mastering the skill that is to be taught. Conditions need to be planned that will help the student focus attention and understand what is required. The strengths and needs list will provide some information about the situations in which the person performs best. Such situations can be considered under a number of headings, as follows.

Times

If there are particular times of the day when a student is more relaxed and able to focus attention, then it will be wise to capitalise on this and use some of this time for teaching. If a student is most alert and attentive in mid-morning before break time, then this would be a good time to choose for structured teaching. Specific reinforcers may vary during the day as to how powerful they are. Thus, if the student is learning how to ask or sign for a drink, it would be best to carry out teaching when the person is likely to be thirsty rather than just after he has already had a drink.

Places

Some skills (for example, undressing) are only appropriate in particular places; others (such as communication) are less 'tied' to this factor. It is important to decide whether the skill to be taught is only relevant in particular places, and to try to carry out teaching in the most naturalistic setting, i.e. the setting in which this skill eventually needs to be practised. Dressing skills may be most appropriately taught in the bedroom (place) when the learner is dressing in the morning (time), and cooking skills in the kitchen during the preparation of the family meal.

Natural settings may sometimes unnecessarily restrict the number of teaching occasions that can occur. There may also be too many distractions in such settings, thus preventing the student from focusing his attention. It may therefore be necessary to carry out initial teaching in a special teaching environment which will cut down the number of distractions and enable more concentrated practice. However, it may still be possible to bring into the arbitrary setting a number of natural setting factors, such as materials or items of equipment, which will help the student associate performance of the skill with more natural settings. The more 'natural' settings factors that can be incorporated into teaching, the greater the likelihood that skills will generalise after learning has occurred. Whatever strategy is adopted, it is important that this be planned in advance by the person carrying out the teaching.

People

It may be that the student responds equally well to most people in the environment, in which case it may not be important to restrict teaching to specific people. Indeed, if skills being taught are ultimately to be practised with a wide range of people (for example, social skills, communication skills), then teaching sessions should be carried out by a variety of individuals so that the student learns to associate usage of the skill with a wide range of people. If skills are ultimately to be practised with, for example, a peer group, then, if possible, peers should be involved in the teaching sessions. If, however, the student is clearly responsive only to particular people, then it may be important to have just these people carry out the teaching, at least in the early stages.

Settings that predispose towards disruptive behaviour

As well as planning for conditions that improve learning, it is necessary to avoid conditions likely to set off behaviours that actively disrupt the teaching process. The same categories are important: times, places and people. If the student is always very restless following a period of free play, then it is important not to try to teach at this time a skill that requires him to sit down and to give his concentrated attention. If the student becomes noisy and agitated in large supermarkets, then it is better to begin learning about shopping skills in a small local shop. If the presence of large numbers of students or staff is often associated with aggression, then it is important to avoid the presence of too many people during teaching occasions.

Step Two Plan triggers

When setting up teaching programmes, three trigger factors need to be considered. These are triggers that focus and maintain the student's attention on the teaching task, triggers that maximise the likelihood of learning, and triggers that may set off problem behaviours.

Triggers that focus attention on the teaching task

Focusing the student's attention on the teaching activity is a prerequisite for effective teaching. There are a number of triggers that can be used to help gain the student's attention:

Verbal instructions. Simple and clear instructions such as 'Look', 'Listen', 'Hands on your lap', can be given at the start of each teaching trial.

Physical guidance. If a student does not respond to verbal cues, then physical prompts such as directing the student's face towards the instructor or task, or directing his hands down on to his lap, can be another effective means of focusing attention on the task.

Materials. The use of materials in teaching which the student finds particularly interesting (for example, a favourite toy, a favourite item of clothing, etc.) can help maintain the student's attention during teaching.

Reinforcers. Another way of gaining and holding the student's attention and interest is to allow him to see and sample at the start of the teaching session the reinforcer which is to be used for correct performance during the session.

When planning teaching it is important not to leave to chance the triggers for gaining the student's attention. By using the same trigger in a consistent manner, the student will learn more quickly what is expected of him.

Triggers that maximise the likelihood of learning

Such triggers, called prompts, can be provided in a number of ways.

Instructions. Explaining to the student in words or gestures what should actually be done.

Demonstration. Showing the student how to perform the task.

Physical guidance. Physically helping the student by guiding his limbs to carry out the task. (In teaching use of a spoon, the teacher might hold a hand over the student's hand so that the spoon is gripped and then guided to the mouth.)

Special equipment. Providing the student with specially adapted materials to simplify learning (for example, using extra large buttons and buttonholes to teach buttoning, padding a spoon handle to assist during eating).

Visual clues. Using non-social visual signals to indicate directly what to do (for example, putting a coloured strip down the back edge of a knife to help indicate which way up to hold it, labelling the back of a vest to help get clothing the right way round when dressing).

These ways are not mutually exclusive and often will be provided in combination. For example, thickening the grip on the spoon handle and providing physical guidance plus instructions such as 'spoon' and 'lift' would be one way of starting off teaching a student to self-feed. But thought needs to be given to the type of prompt that most suits the individual student. Demonstrating a task to a student who rarely looks in the direction of the teacher or who does not show evidence of imitative skills is unlikely to be useful. Explaining in sentences what should be done can only be helpful if the student has some understanding of language. Physical guidance may lead to physical resistance from some students. Thus, in planning the use of prompts, it is essential to choose triggers that are useful on an individual basis to the student.

Selecting appropriate level of prompt

As well as planning whether to use prompts and, if so, what sort, it is also essential to plan the level of help needed. If too much help is given, the student may come to depend entirely on prompting and learn nothing about the task itself. If too little help is given, the student may make errors and fail to learn altogether or learn inappropriate behaviours.

Prompts can be broken down into a series of steps in the same way as the tasks themselves can (see Section Three). As an example, a physical prompt used to help a student lift a spoon can be broken down into the following steps:

(1) Holding hand over student's hand and guiding to mouth.
(2) Holding hand over student's hand and guiding until 1 inch from mouth (student completes task unaided).
(3) Guidance until 3 inches from mouth.
(4) Moving guidance from holding student's hand to holding forearm and guiding arm to mouth.
(5) As for (4) but removing guidance 1 inch from mouth.
(6) As for (4) but removing guidance 6 inches from mouth.
(7) Moving guidance from forearm to elbow and guiding to mouth.
(8) As for (7) but removing guidance 6 inches from mouth.
(9) Student lifts spoon to mouth independently.

When determining the level of prompt to be used, it is important to use the *minimum* amount of prompting needed to *ensure correct performance* of the skill: thus the student should perform the task correctly but with as much active personal contribution as possible.

Triggers that set off disruptive behaviours

Disruptive behaviours are triggered just like any other behaviour. In skill teaching it is important to exclude triggers that will set off problem behaviours and thus interfere with the learning process. If a student is always aggressive towards a particular peer (the trigger), then this peer should not be involved in the teaching programme. If certain materials (for example, those that scatter or break into small pieces) reliably trigger throwing, then these should not be available in the teaching situation. If a student has a particular fear (such as of the colour red) and becomes very distressed in the presence of a feared object, then the object should be excluded from the teaching situation.

In this context it is important to consider the use of the word 'No'. *No* is used as a way of making somebody stop what they are doing. It is supposed to trigger a halt on the basis that if the person does not stop, something unpleasant will follow. It may trigger general 'freezing', or anxiety and avoidance which may include aggression. None of these behaviours is useful in a learning situation. A trigger such as 'no' should therefore be kept out of skill teaching programmes.

Step Three *Plan results*

There are two kinds of result which need to be planned for in a skill teaching programme. The first are *reinforcers*, which should occur when the skill is performed correctly. The second are *reminders*, which should occur when errors are made.

Reinforcers

Selecting a reinforcer

In planning how to use reinforcement in a skill teaching programme, it is important to consider first the natural reinforcer for the skill in question and to use this whenever possible. For example, the natural reinforcer for a greeting response (e.g. 'Hello') would be a reciprocal greeting and perhaps a smile. The natural reinforcer for requesting an object would be the object itself. The natural reinforcer for having a bath would be a feeling of freshness and, perhaps, the pleasant smell of soap or talcum powder. Whenever possible the natural reinforcer should be used. However, if the natural reinforcer cannot be delivered immediately (for example, the natural reinforcer for planting seeds would be the sight of flowers blooming in that place several weeks or months later), or if it is unlikely to be meaningful for the student (not all individuals find the attention or smiles of others meaningful or pleasant), then it will be necessary to select an arbitrary reinforcer which can be given immediately and which is powerful enough to act as a source of encouragement. The student's strengths and needs list will provide information on such effective reinforcers.

Using a reinforcer

A reinforcer will have its greatest strengthening effect on the behaviour which immediately precedes it in time. It is therefore best for a reinforcer to *follow immediately* the student's action. In the early stages of learning, the reinforcer should follow the action *on every occasion* that the skill is performed correctly.

Reminders

In addition to planning a response for correct performance, a response should also be planned for errors. As already mentioned it

65

is important to avoid strategies that might punish the student (such as 'no, that's wrong'): this will introduce anxiety and avoidance into the learning situation. The most useful way to respond is to provide the student with information about what should have been done: what was the correct response. In the STAR system, these tactics are called reminders.

Selecting a reminder

Reminders are provided in two main ways:

Demonstration. The teacher demonstrates what was the correct response and then encourages the student to try again. Thus if the student learning colour matching puts a red with a blue object, the teacher would demonstrate the correct match and then offer the student another red object to sort.

Extra help. If a student cannot imitate, or if the task is difficult to demonstrate, then an alternative way of reminding is to take the student through the task with enough extra help to ensure success. For example, if a student drops the spoon when lifting from the plate, the teacher might repeat the scoop and lift sequence but with enough physical help to ensure success.

Difficulties can sometimes arise with some students who find such demonstration or extra help reinforcing. They may find it quite entertaining to see somebody doing the task for them or giving them a lot of extra physical help. They may therefore continue to make errors just to get this kind of result (reminders become reinforcers). If this occurs, then two further strategies can be used:

Interruption. Without comment, the teacher interrupts the student and restarts the whole task.

Ignoring. If the teacher is quite certain that the student can do the task, then all attention can be withheld until the task is completed satisfactorily. If this strategy is adopted, it is important to remember that no attention must be given until the student responds correctly: the teacher must be prepared to wait as long as it takes, otherwise the student learns that persisting long enough in an error finally leads to attention. For this reason, ignoring is a strategy of last resort.

Using a reminder

As with reinforcers, reminders should occur very quickly after the error, However, it may be important to allow for an element of discovery learning if the student is able to self-correct an error. Thus, if the student makes an attempt to correct his own mistake, then up to a minute can be allowed before reminding. If the student continues to pursue the same mistake (for example, keeps trying to put the circle in the square hole of a shape-sorting box), then a reminder should occur more quickly, within 10 seconds. If the problem is more one of the student's making no response at all, then a fixed number of seconds (5–20) should be allowed before demonstration or extra help is given. Ignoring is obviously a rather different strategy and needs to be used in the way described above.

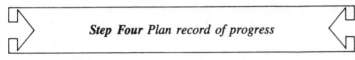

Step Four *Plan record of progress*

When teaching new skills it is essential to record the progress which is being made in skill learning, to judge whether the programme is leading to improvements in the student's level of competence.

What to record

The simplest way of judging progress is to measure whether a student carried out a skill or not. This is a two-way system of measurement — Yes/No — Did the student cross the road in the right place? Did he lift the spoon to his mouth; butter the toast; ask for help when in difficulty? Progress is occurring if the number of times that the answer is 'yes' is increasing. Whilst this is a simple measure, it is relatively insensitive to progress for students with severe learning disabilities. As outlined in Step Two, the STAR approach to teaching is usually to ensure minimum errors by providing enough help to guarantee success. Thus, a more sensitive way to monitor progress is to record whether or not the student needed extra help when practising the skill. Did the student . . . cross at the right place without verbal prompts, with verbal prompts, not at all? . . . lift the spoon to the mouth without any help, with physical prompts from the elbow, with physical prompts from the wrist, with physical prompts from the hand, not at all? The more detailed the measure, the more sensitive it will be to changes, but the more complex and time consuming it will be to carry out.

How to record

During skill training, recording should be carried out at the same time as the teaching. If recording is left to the end of a teaching session, or if there is any time delay between the teaching and the recording, then the likelihood of mistakes increases. Recording may be carried out every time a task is presented (continuous recording) or only on selected occasions (sample recording) (see Section Eight) but it should always accompany the teaching itself. In order to do this it will be necessary to draw up a recording chart which will accompany the written programme instructions. Such a chart is best laid out so that the student's performance over time can be seen. The bottom of the chart should be divided up into sections of time (days of the week, sessions of teaching). The vertical part of the chart should be divided into the occasions of teaching within each time period (the trials within each session, the occasions within each day). Figure 4.2 provides an example of a simple recording chart.

Figure 4.2: Simple recording chart for skill teaching

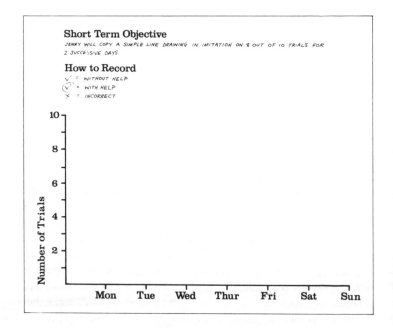

Different ways of drawing up recording charts and different types of symbol which can be used to represent the student's level of performance, so that each possible outcome is represented by a different symbol, are illustrated in Figure 4.3.

How to analyse

Judgement of progress depends upon an examination of the records. This is much easier where the records are contained on a single sheet as illustrated in Figure 4.3. This allows the assessment of progress at a glance, particularly if the visual symbols are very different from each other. The comparison is of the changes taking place since the baseline measures (see Section Eight).

When teaching new skills which are relevant to problem behaviour management, it may also be important to monitor spontaneous usage of the skill by the student and also to measure the impact of the new skill on the problem behaviour. Planning how to record these aspects of skill learning is discussed in Sections Five and Six, respectively.

 Step Five Plan to consolidate learning

When planning teaching programmes that involve the use of arbitrary STAR factors, it is important also to plan ways of helping students consolidate learning and of making new skills more broadly useful. Three common ways of doing this are:

(a) Informing other people about the broad aim of a teaching programme and asking them to do their best to encourage the same sort of skill. Whilst a student might be involved at a day facility in a systematic programme to learn buttoning skills, relatives and friends might be asked more generally to get the student to do as much as possible of his buttoning.

(b) Introducing the same concepts less formally with different materials. A student might be working on a systematic programme to learn basic colours using a specific set of materials, but others who know the student could be asked to comment on these colours in every-day situations (for example, in relation to clothes or food).

(c) Introducing the same skills on different occasions. A student might be learning in specific sessions how to ask for items by name. If these same items are available at other times of the day,

Figure 4.3: Examples of techniques for recording progress in skill learning

A. Yes/No Records

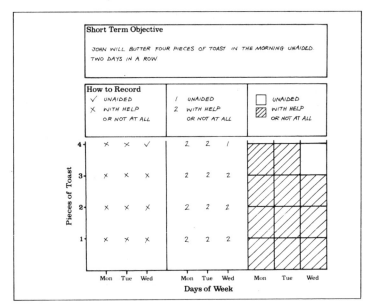

B. Unaided/With Help/Not at all · Records

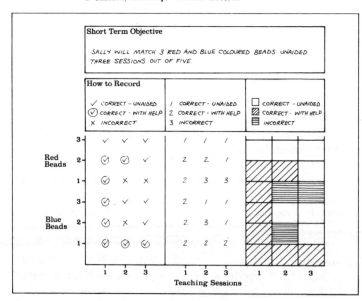

Figure 4.3: *Continued*

C. Unaided/Physical Guidance (P.G.) from elbow/P.G. from wrist/
P.G. from hand/Not at all - Record

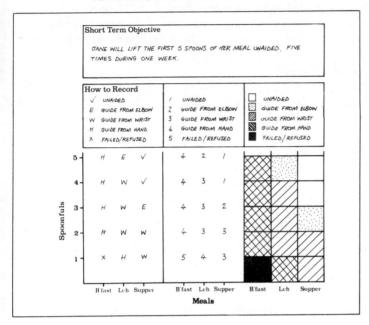

Short Term Objective
JANE WILL LIFT THE FIRST 5 SPOONS OF HER MEAL UNAIDED, FIVE TIMES DURING ONE WEEK.

then the requirement to ask could be introduced into these other occasions.

Such practice in skill usage is important for consolidating new learning and should be built into a teaching plan. It helps to prevent learning becoming too specific, and some students helped in this way will readily generalise their learning without more systematic and time-consuming approaches.

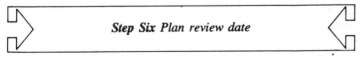

Step Six Plan review date

A date must be specified on which the programme will be reviewed to judge whether it should be continued, changed or abandoned. Such a date should occur within four weeks of the start of the programme and be part of a regular ongoing process of programme review.

Step Seven *Write a skill teaching programme*

Having decided on each aspect of the skill programme, the next step is to write down the details in the form of a written programme. A written skill building programme should include the following details:

Long-term goal
This is a statement about the longer term aim of the programme: what it is hoped the student will achieve over the coming few months (Section Three, Step One).

Short-term objective
This is a detailed statement about the immediate aim of the programme. It will state: *Who* will do *what* under what *circumstances* to what *degree of success* (Section Three, Step Four).

Time and place of session
If a specific time and place have been allocated for teaching, then these must be specified (Step One).

People involved
If only certain people are to carry out teaching, these need to be named. If several people are to carry out teaching, this should also be specified (Step One).

Special materials
Specific materials used for teaching must be described and itemised (Step Two).

Number of teaching trials per session
Where appropriate, a statement needs to be made about the number of times the teaching procedure is to be repeated in each session.

Procedure
This must include the following details:

(a) method of gaining the student's attention (Step Two),
(b) manner of presenting the task to the student (Step Two),
(c) prompting strategy to be used to help student complete the task (Step Two).

Response to appropriate behaviour
This involves details of the type and method of reinforcement for correct performance of the skill (Step Three).

Response to inappropriate behaviour
These are details of reminders to be used when errors occur (Step Three).

Consolidation strategy
This provides details of where and how to practise the skill being taught in more natural situations (Step Five).

Recording
Details must be provided of how to record performance, including a prepared recording chart (Step Four).

Date of review
(Step Six)

An example of a written skill teaching programme is illustrated in Figure 4.4.

Step Eight *Moving on*

When the short-term objective has been achieved, a decision has to be made about how to extend the teaching. This requires consideration of the two goals of teaching: skill mastery and generalised skill usage.

Moving towards skill mastery

The first phase of teaching will require moving through a series of short-term objectives until the long-term teaching goal has been achieved. The short-term objectives will have been largely planned at the start of teaching following the task analysis, and a decision will have been made about the organisation of teaching (part-task or whole-task teaching, backward or forward chaining, shaping). Each part of the task will probably need to be taught using arbitrary triggers in the form of prompts. Each type of prompt will itself be graded along a number of levels (see Step Two). Thus, moving towards skill mastery is done using the principle of graded change to (a) reduce the level of prompting in a systematic way at each stage of learning (if several kinds of prompt are being used, then each needs to be

73

Figure 4.4: Example of skill teaching programme

Name JULIE	**Date** APRIL 22ND

Long Term Goal JULIE WILL OPERATE THE TAPE RECORDER INDEPENDENTLY (INSERT TAPE; PRESS, PLAY, STOP, REWIND AS NECESSARY)

Short Term Objective

JULIE WILL FIND AND PRESS THE 'PLAY' BUTTON ON THE TAPE RECORDER ONCE A TAPE HAS BEEN INSERTED FOR HER, 3 TIMES OUT OF 4 ON 5 CONSECUTIVE SESSIONS.

People Involved

WHOEVER IS ALLOCATED TO WORK WITH JULIE ON THE EVENING SHIFT.

Time & Place AFTER SUPPER IN HER OWN ROOM

Special Materials	**Trials per Session**
JULIE'S TAPE RECORDER WITH A RED LABEL STUCK OVER THE 'PLAY' BUTTON; HER 3 FAVOURITE TAPES.	4

Procedure

ONCE EVERYONE HAS FINISHED SUPPER, TELL JULIE YOU'RE GOING TO HELP HER LEARN HOW TO WORK THE TAPE RECORDER. ASK HER TO GO WITH YOU TO FIND IT. WHEN SHE'S GOT THE TAPE RECORDER OUT, ASK HER WHICH OF HER FAVOURITE TAPES SHE WOULD LIKE TO LISTEN TO.

GET HER ATTENTION BY SAYING "LOOK, JULIE, WATCH HOW I PUT THE TAPE IN." WHEN SHE IS LOOKING, INSERT TAPE, THEN SAY "NOW YOU PRESS THE PLAY BUTTON."

Response to Appropriate Behaviour

AS SOON AS SHE PRESSES THE CORRECT BUTTON, PRAISE HER ENTHUSIASTICALLY AND LET HER LISTEN TO HER TAPE FOR 2-3 MINUTES. THEN TURN TAPE OFF SAYING "LET'S SEE IF YOU CAN FIND THE 'PLAY' BUTTON AGAIN (REPEAT 2 MORE TIMES FOR A TOTAL OF 4 TRIES)

Response to Inappropriate Behaviour

① IF JULIE PRESSES THE WRONG BUTTON, TURN IT OFF, POINT TO THE RIGHT ONE SAYING "LOOK, IT'S THIS BUTTON, THE ONE UNDER THE RED STICKER." ② IF SHE STILL DOES NOT PRESS THE RIGHT BUTTON TAKE HER FINGER IN YOUR HAND AND PHYSICALLY PROMPT HER TO PRESS THE CORRECT ONE, SAYING "THIS IS THE 'PLAY' BUTTON, THE ONE UNDER THE RED STICKER." ③ IF JULIE REFUSES TO PRESS THE RIGHT BUTTON, REMOVE TAPE FROM RECORDER SAYING "LET'S TRY AGAIN WATCH HOW I PUT THE TAPE IN... NOW YOU PRESS THE 'PLAY' BUTTON" (REPEAT PROMPT SEQUENCE AS ABOVE).

Generalisation

WHENEVER THE OPPORTUNITY ARISES TO TURN ON A TAPE OR VIDEO RECORDER, INVITE JULIE TO COME AND TURN IT ON.

Recording RECORD FOR EACH OF 4 TRIALS: ✓: CORRECT RESPONSE UNAIDED Ⓥ: CORRECT RESPONSE USING VERBAL PROMPT Ⓟ: CORRECT RESPONSE USING PHYSICAL PROMPT X = FAILURE	**Date of Review** MAY 6TH

Table 4.1: Moving on towards long-term goals through graded change

---

Long-term goal: Mary will let people know what she wants by leading them to an object and pointing to it.

Short-term objectives:

(1) When asked what she wants, Mary will move arm in direction of object with physical guidance from wrist
(2) As (1) with physical guidance from elbow
(3) As (1) with light touch to elbow
(4) As (1) with no help
(5) When asked what she wants, Mary will move arm in direction of object, index finger pointed with physical help to point finger
(6) As (5) with reminder (demonstration) to point
(7) With adult 5 feet from object, Mary will take hold of adult's arm and lead to object with physical prompt, then point to what she wants as in (6)
(8) As (7) with no help
(9) As (8) with adult 8 feet from object
(10) As (8) with different adults present
(11) As (8) with adults outside room

---

reduced similarly in a systematic and gradual fashion); (b) increase the proportion of the task which the student is required to complete in order to obtain reinforcement.

Table 4.1 illustrates how the principle of graded change is used to take the student through a series of short-term objectives involving reducing prompts at each stage and systematically increasing the amount which the student must do to obtain reinforcement. In the example given, a part-task, backward-chaining procedure has been used.

Moving towards generalised usage of the skill

Skills learned in the presence of arbitrary settings, triggers and results may not generalise spontaneously to natural situations. This may be because the student has not been provided with clues as to the appropriate settings in which to use the skill. He may not, for example, have learned to recognise the natural triggers while prompts were being used. In addition, the natural results for performance of the skills may be quite different from the powerful and frequent reinforcers used in the early stages of teaching. Encouraging students informally to consolidate learning by practising new skills in a variety of situations (Step Six) may go some way to overcoming these difficulties. However, a more systematic generalisation procedure may need to be adopted if this informal approach is not effective.

Introducing natural settings

This involves using the principle of graded change to introduce natural setting factors into formal teaching situations. These setting factors include places, prompts and materials.

Places. If teaching has had to take place in special teaching environments, it should be possible early on to bring into this 'arbitrary' setting a number of 'natural' setting factors, such as equipment, materials or even items of furniture, which belong to the setting where skills ultimately need to be practised in order to provide the student with clues about when it will be appropriate to use his newly learned skill. If the skill does not generalise to natural situations, teaching sessions may need to be moved to the natural places in which they will ultimately need to be practised as the student begins to master the skill. This may require practising the skill systematically in a number of different places.

People. If the skill being taught is one that needs to be used in the presence of a wide range of people (e.g. social skills), then again the principle of graded change can be used to introduce new people into the teaching situation as learning progresses. These new people may need to be representative of those in whose presence the skills will need to be performed (for example, peers).

Materials. Introducing variations of the task to be learned is another way of promoting generalisation. For example, once a child has been taught to push along a car, a number of toys on wheels could be systematically introduced into the formal teaching situation as a way of encouraging generalised usage of this play skill.

Fading out arbitrary triggers

Gradually fading out arbitrary triggers is one way to help the student start to notice and respond to natural triggers. In this way the prompt is broken down into levels (Step Two) and the level of prompting is systematically reduced. In the final stages it may be useful to delay prompting by several seconds as a way of encouraging students to respond to the natural trigger.

Fading out arbitrary reinforcers

As a skill becomes more practised, so the principle of graded change should be used to decrease the frequency of reinforcement. Following an earlier example, when a child first starts to use a potty he is praised and fussed over on each occasion that he 'performs'. Once he has started to use the potty regularly, praise will no longer be given on every occasion. When decreasing the frequency of reinforcement, it is best to do this in a way which introduces some *unpredictability* as to the exact times when the reinforcer follows the action. In decreasing praise for use of the potty from every time to every other time, it is better not to do this by simply alternating praise and no praise, but by making the decision on a more unpredictable basis, for example, by the spin of a coin. Decreasing the frequency and increasing the unpredictability of reinforcement is a powerful way of helping students continue to work at skill learning tasks. If arbitrary reinforcement is used, it is a way of shifting control to more natural events.

When planning the teaching of new skills it is important early on to consider how to 'move on' through the different stages towards spontaneous skill usage. Clearly, specific decisions about how to do this will need to be part of the ongoing review of programmes, and will depend to some extent on the speed with which the student moves towards skill mastery. 'Moving on' towards spontaneous skill usage should never be taken for granted. If informal strategies to consolidate learning prove ineffective, then the teacher needs to plan more systematic ways of helping the student to move on. Again, this will be part of the ongoing review of progress.

Carrying out skill teaching programmes

A systematic approach to teaching new skills, as described in the preceding steps, represents a highly effective form of teaching. Even so, progress is not always easy, and carrying out such teaching can be hard work and time consuming. This is particularly true when working with people who have serious behavioural difficulties. Having a systematic programme is also no guarantee that it will be carried out. There are many general factors that contribute to whether or not constructive help is provided for students with severe behavioural difficulties. These are more fully discussed in Section Nine. However, as regards skill teaching, a number of practical hints can be offered which will help teachers carry out programmes efficiently and regularly.

Providing organised teaching

The effectiveness of a high-quality teaching programme depends, to

77

a large extent, on how well it is carried out. From a practical point of view, a few simple rules, if followed, should help maximise the likelihood of success and provide encouragement to continue.

Preparing the session fully before engaging the student

The student should never be kept waiting while the teacher prepares the teaching session or interrupts the session to collect forgotten materials, as he may become discouraged or bored waiting and then be less eager to co-operate with teaching. The teacher should ensure that teaching materials are prepared, recording forms and pencils are available, and programme details, including instructions, reinforcers and details of correction procedures, are fully understood. If several people are to be involved in the teaching, it is useful to run through the programme together at an early stage, using modelling and role play, to ensure details are understood by all concerned.

Staying in control during the session

The teacher should have control over all aspects of the teaching situation — including materials and reinforcers. Unwilling students have been known to tip tables and chairs, destroy teaching materials, tear up recording forms and consume all reinforcers before a session has even begun! Reinforcers should, as a general rule, be kept out of reach of the student. If they are a source of distraction, they may also need to be kept out of sight and produced only when the desired response occurs. In certain extreme cases, it may be difficult for one person to keep control of materials and equipment and also to prompt a student through correct performance of a task. In such cases, a helper can be enlisted so that the teacher can maintain full control over the session with a helper providing back-up for prompting, handling materials and recording.

Finishing sessions on a note of success

To increase the likelihood that the student and teacher will enjoy the teaching situation, it is important that the sessions always end with success. This may sometimes mean allowing the student a final attempt which is over-prompted, or decreasing the level of demand for the final trial, in order to ensure success. Finishing on a note of failure can be discouraging for the student and decreases willingness to co-operate in subsequent sessions. It can also be discouraging for the teacher and can decrease readiness to allocate time for teaching on subsequent occasions.

Providing regular teaching

For people with serious learning difficulties, teaching needs to be delivered on a regular and frequent basis if measurable progress in learning is to occur. Specific and focused skill teaching programmes such as those described in this section, should be carried out at least daily for the student to gain maximum benefit from them. This can be a difficult goal to achieve. Other priorities such as unforeseen crises and meetings, and more exciting activities such as outings, can easily fill a day so that no time is left for individual teaching. Yet, if a long-term solution to behaviour problems is to be achieved, then teaching must be carried out regularly and such regular teaching efforts need to be sustained over a long period of time. It is easier to intervene directly with unacceptable behaviours because the student's behaviour acts as a trigger for a response from others, ensuring that some action is taken. As regards teaching, however, the student usually provides no prompt to those around him. The onus is on the teacher to provide his own reminders which will ensure that teaching is carried out. Although there is no right or easy answer to how this might be achieved, nevertheless there are a number of ways by which the probability of providing regular and frequent teaching can be increased:

(a) Timetabling teaching times into the day will increase the likelihood that these times are not taken up by other matters.
(b) Allocating named people to carry out teaching on specific days will give people direct and personal responsibility for teaching.
(c) Ensuring that in the absence of key people some other named person is made responsible for organising the teaching time-table.
(d) Ensuring that written teaching programmes, recording forms and all necessary materials for teaching are kept available in a central location to avoid time wasting during the time set aside for a teaching session.
(e) Alternatively, publicly posting up teaching programmes in the relevant teaching area to act as visual prompts to carry out teaching.
(f) Ensuring that recording is kept up to date.
(g) Ensuring that review dates for programmes are strictly adhered to so that problems in programme implementation can be discussed and resolved.
(h) Regularly reviewing long-term aims and objectives to remind

everyone about the purpose of the teaching and to sustain motivation to continue.

(i) Publicly 'celebrating' any teaching success.

There are undoubtedly many other tactics which can be used to help teachers persevere with structured teaching programmes, but the above at least provides a few starting points.

SUMMARY

Teaching important alternative skills is an essential component of problem behaviour management. By definition, people with serious learning disabilities find new learning difficult and thus teaching them new skills takes time. To simplify learning, teaching needs to be structured to minimise the likelihood of errors by carefully controlling settings, triggers and results and by using a systematic and graded approach. This requires accurate record keeping and close monitoring of progress so that the student can be 'moved on' towards long-term goals. Having mastered new skills, it cannot be assumed that these will automatically be used in conditions other than those present during training, and steps may need to be taken to help the student generalise his newly learned skill to relevant new situations.

In this section, the general principles of skill teaching have been utilised. Specific steps have been described which, if systematically followed, can help the reader move from the assessment stage described in Section Two and the planning of specific teaching goals described in Section Three to planning, writing and implementing programmes which will achieve these goals in the area of new skill teaching.

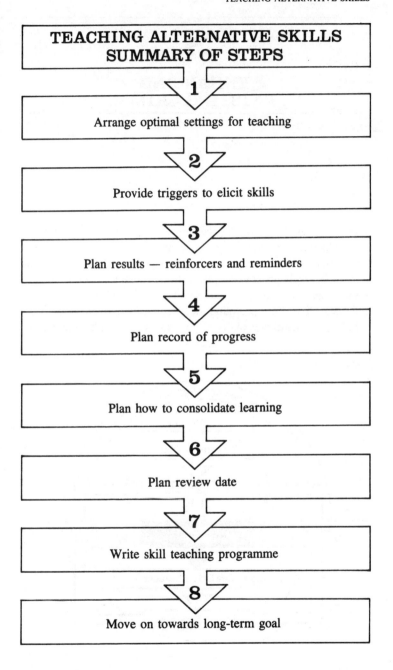

TEACHING ALTERNATIVE SKILLS
SUMMARY OF STEPS

1

Arrange optimal settings for teaching

2

Provide triggers to elicit skills

3

Plan results — reinforcers and reminders

4

Plan record of progress

5

Plan how to consolidate learning

6

Plan review date

7

Write skill teaching programme

8

Move on towards long-term goal

5

ENHANCING
EXISTING SKILLS

In the previous section the procedures for selecting and teaching new skills which are relevant to behaviour management were discussed. New skills, however, may take a very long time to learn. They may need to be built up slowly, in small steps, then generalised in a graded way if they are to occur spontaneously and be useful to the individual. The more profound the learning impairment, the longer it will take to learn new skills. If a person has multiple impairments

Figure 5.1

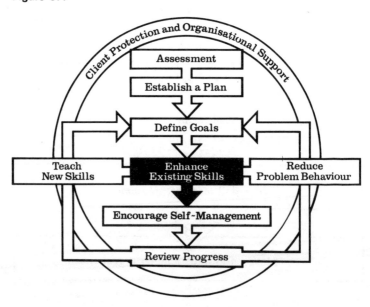

(behavioural, sensory or neurological), then learning may be further impaired. Learning new skills can be a problem also for people who suffer from a specific learning disability in addition to their general impairment. Thus, for example, progress in communication skills will be slower for people who have a language disorder than for those who do not, even though they may make progress in other areas. For a number of individuals, therefore, progress in learning important new skills which can contribute to the reduction of their problem behaviours may be extremely slow. For these individuals in particular it is important to consider the skills which they already possess but rarely use. Enhancing and extending existing skills is likely to achieve faster results than teaching new skills.

A. GENERAL PRINCIPLES FOR ENHANCING SKILLS

Understanding why skills are not practised

Everyone, no matter how severe their disability, has a range of actions which are potentially available for use: reaching, grasping, lifting, looking, sitting and vocalising are just some examples. Most individuals can use their skills for a range of important activities: to occupy themselves, to communicate their needs, to comply with requests, to join in group activities, and to do things for themselves. For a number of reasons, however, these skills may be practised only infrequently, if at all.

In the first place, the opportunities to practise specific skills may be unavailable. For example, a person may be able to prepare some foods for cooking or be able to wash up, but may be unable to show these skills because he is not allowed into the kitchen. Alternatively, even if allowed into the kitchen, the individual may appear quite incompetent at cooking if there is an electric stove and he has been taught to cook with gas. A child may have a number of play skills but cannot show them if no toys are available or if the wrong kinds of toy are available. Thus, a child who is skilled with rattles and squeaky toys may be unable to play when surrounded by Lego bricks.

Restricted access to places or materials is one way in which opportunities to practise skills are denied. Another way is when, for the sake of convenience, other people perform specific skills on the individual's behalf. Thus, although a person may be able to choose between activities or indicate if he does not want to do something, other people may make the choices and decisions for him. A child who is able to dress himself independently may be dressed each morning in order to ensure that he does not keep the school bus waiting when it arrives. A person may be fed his meals in order not to delay the rest of the group going out for a walk.

Another important reason why skills are not practised is that they do not achieve any meaningful *results* for the person. In other words, the skills are not reinforced. A person may be able to ask for a drink but will not do so very often if, whenever he asks, he is told to wait until it is 'time'. A child may be able to play alone for several minutes but will not do so if, whenever he engages in play activities, he is 'left alone' or ignored. An adult may be able to lift and stack objects but may not enjoy practising these skills using coloured plastic bricks (using these same skills to help unpack and put away the shopping in the kitchen may provide far greater satisfaction).

It has been suggested earlier in this book that behaviour problems should be regarded as meaningful and skilled actions which achieve important results for the individual. Appropriate skills may be used infrequently because they achieve only weak or occasional results. In contrast, inappropriate skills may be achieving powerful results for the individual. This is known as *differential reinforcement*. It is an important concept to understand. When a person has a number of possible actions, each of which is associated with different types and strengths of reinforcement, he will tend to behave in a way that gets the best 'return', in other words, that achieves the most reinforcement. For example, a child may find that when he cries and scratches himself someone will sit him on their lap and comfort him, but when he tries to sit on their lap at other times, he is sent away. When this happens, the process of differential reinforcement is in operation. The frequency of crying and scratching will increase and the frequency of approaching people will decrease. A person may find that when he sits quietly at the dinner table waiting for a staff member to come and cut up his food he is frequently left to the end so that his food gets cold. When, on the other hand, he throws his cutlery across the room or screams, someone immediately comes to attend to his needs. This is another example of the process of differential reinforcement in operation. The frequency of screaming and throwing at mealtimes will increase and the frequency of sitting quietly and waiting will decrease. To give one final example, a person may find that if he pushes someone gently to move them away they usually ignore him and stay where they are. If, however, he bites or scratches them they immediately move away. Here again the process of differential reinforcement is at work. The frequency of appropriately asking people to move away will decrease and the frequency of biting and scratching will increase. Such comparisons of returns do not have to take place at a conscious level. They simply occur through experience of the different results for different actions.

Techniques for enhancing skills

Differential reinforcement

If appropriate skills are used infrequently because they do not achieve meaningful results, and inappropriate actions, because they achieve immediate results, are used in their place, then, by altering the comparative results for these behaviours, appropriate skills can be built up and inappropriate behaviours decreased. This is achieved using techniques based upon the principle of differential reinforcement, i.e. non-reinforcement of inappropriate behaviours (see Section Six) and reinforcement of important alternative skills. The three major strategies for using this approach are:

(a) Differential reinforcement of other behaviours (DRO) — all skills other than the problem behaviour.
(b) Differential reinforcement of equivalent behaviours (DRE) — skills which serve the same function as the problem behaviour.
(c) Differential reinforcement of incompatible behaviour (DRI) — skills which cannot be performed at the same time as the problem behaviour.

DRO differs from DRI or DRE in one major respect. DRI and DRE are both response-based strategies. In other words, the performance by the individual of specific, predefined behaviours results in re-inforcement, regardless of the frequency with which they occur. It is the client's *response* which determines whether reinforcement occurs. DRO, on the other hand, is a *time*-based strategy. *All* skills other than the problem behaviour are considered appropriate and, hence, reinforcible. In other words, it is the absence of the problem behaviour which determines whether reinforcement occurs. Re-inforcement is delivered contingent on a predetermined time interval, during which the inappropriate behaviour does not occur. The length of the time interval is, to a large extent, determined by the usual frequency of the problem behaviour. Reinforcement is planned in such a way that it occurs more frequently than does the inappropriate behaviour, thereby ensuring that the pay-off for appropriate behaviours is greater than any pay-off received by the inappropriate action.

A full assessment of the person's skills and problem behaviours will highlight which strategy will be the most useful one to adopt. having selected the most appropriate strategy it is important, next, to ensure that the desired actions are performed in place of inappropriate ones and that they achieve powerful results for the individual when they do occur.

Use of arbitrary STAR factors

In Section Four the distinction between 'arbitrary' and 'natural' STAR factors was made. Arbitrary events are special events which need to be introduced into a teaching situation in order that learning may occur, but which would not occur normally in the natural environment.

In every-day life, actions are triggered by specific events. Thus, finishing a meal may be the trigger for putting the knife and fork down on to the plate; wanting attention may be the trigger for going up to another person and starting to talk with them; finding oneself with nothing to do may be the trigger for turning on the television. For people with serious learning disabilities, other less acceptable responses may have become associated with environmental triggers, through different learning and reinforcement histories. In this way, finishing a meal may have become the trigger for throwing the plate on to the floor, wanting attention may have become the trigger for screaming or hitting, finding oneself with nothing to do may have become the trigger for head weaving or for rocking.

In order to encourage the individual to use appropriate skills in place of inappropriate behaviours which are achieving positive results for him, it may be necessary, at least initially, to introduce arbitrary reinforcers which are powerful and which occur frequently so that appropriate behaviours are made a more attractive option than the inappropriate actions. Then, in order to give the student the opportunity of experiencing reinforcement for his appropriate behaviours, arbitrary triggers in the form of prompts may also need to be used in these early stages.

Graded change

Once appropriate actions are occurring frequently and reliably, arbitrary triggers and results need to be faded out, through the process of graded change described in Section Four. The process of graded change is used to move the student towards responding to natural triggers and results by gradually and systematically decreasing prompts and reducing the frequency of arbitrary reinforcers in a step-by-step manner until natural STAR factors are maintaining behaviour. Abrupt withdrawal of prompts or arbitrary reinforcers is likely to result in skills again being used only infrequently or not at all.

The first part of this section has outlined the general principles involved in enhancing existing skills as a way of managing problem behaviours. These involve analysis of and attention to STAR factors which surround the individual and influence his behaviours. Having outlined the general principles, the second part of this section will detail the specific steps required to develop effective programmes for enhancing existing skills.

B. DEVELOPING PROGRAMMES FOR ENHANCING SKILLS

The strengths and needs list (Section Two) will have summarised the learning needs of the individual that are considered important for the long-term resolution of the problem behaviour. These should include skills which the person already possesses but rarely performs. These skills might be expected to have a significant impact on the problem behaviour if they occurred more frequently and consistently. From the statement of needs a long-term goal will have been established and this will have been broken down into a series of achievable steps from which more immediate short-term objectives will have been set (Section Three). Having done this, a programme for achieving these objectives can then be formulated.

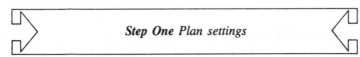

Step One Plan settings

The first step is to ensure that the settings in which the skills are to be encouraged are organised in a way which maximises the likelihood of their being practised. This requires determining the situations in which the skills need to occur and then ensuring that opportunities to practise the skills are made available in these situations.

87

Providing opportunities

Providing opportunities may mean providing access to materials. For example, if a student is to be encouraged to keep his hands in his pockets rather than slap his face, then all the clothes which he wears should be fitted with large, easily accessible pockets. If a student is to be encouraged to chew on a plastic or rubber 'chew' instead of his fingers, then the 'chew' may need to be made permanently available by being fixed to the clothing or worn around the neck. If a child is being encouraged to use his play skills during unstructured periods, then he should have easy access to toys and equipment during these times — perhaps by being provided with his own special 'toy box' which contains his favourite toys.

In certain situations, providing opportunities may mean allowing the individual access to a wider range of activities to enable him to practise his skills more. For example, if an individual likes water and knows how to wash pots and pans, then, unless there is a good reason, he should be allowed into the kitchen to help. In other situations, providing opportunities may mean allowing a student greater access to people. Thus, if social or communication skills are being encouraged, then it may be necessary to structure the environment so that time is made available for carers to spend time simply chatting to the student or sharing activities with him, to provide him with the opportunity to practise relevant skills.

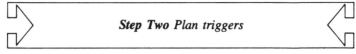

Step Two *Plan triggers*

Having provided opportunities which enable the student to practise relevant skills, the next step is to plan ways of ensuring that the student practises these skills.

Determining the need for extra triggers

Additional triggers or prompts are not always necessary when using differential reinforcement to build up existing skills. In particular, when using a time-based strategy in programmes where *all* behaviours other than the problem behaviour are being encouraged (DRO), there is likely to be ample opportunity to reinforce the student for not engaging in the problem behaviour, particularly if settings have been planned so as to provide maximum opportunities for practising positive skills. A different situation arises when using a response-based strategy, that is, when specific skills which are either incompatible with (DRI) or functionally equivalent to (DRE) the problem behaviour are being encouraged, since these skills need to occur in place of the unacceptable behaviour, in other words, at very specific times. In such cases a prompt will need to be provided to ensure that the student carries out the appropriate skill at the appropriate time.

Selecting suitable prompts

There are a number of prompts that can be used to encourage an individual to use his skills. The most frequently used prompts are the following:

Suggestion. This involves using words or gestures to remind the person what the appropriate behaviour should be.

Demonstration. This involves showing the individual what he should be doing.

Physical guidance. This means physically prompting the individual through the required action. Even though a person may already know how to perform a skill, this type of prompt may be necessary in order to pre-empt performance of an inappropriate behaviour and to allow him to experience reinforcement.

Selection of the appropriate prompt will depend to a large extent on the action being encouraged. As an example, getting the individual involved in listening to music may require that the teacher sit down himself for a while to listen to the music in order to encourage the student to do the same (demonstration). Getting a student to push his plate gently to one side instead of throwing it on to the floor may require a physical prompt in order to pre-empt the inappropriate action. Getting the person to ask for help with a piece of work may require a verbal reminder at the appropriate time.

Timing the prompt

Timing prompts is very important. Arbitrary triggers are dependent

89

to a large extent on the occurrence of natural triggers. Sometimes they need to coincide with the natural triggers. This is particularly important for skills which serve the same function as the problem behaviour. The prompt must be timed in such a way as to pre-empt performance of the inappropriate action and to teach the person to respond with a different action to the natural trigger. For example, if a child throws equipment in order to gain his teacher's attention when he has finished a piece of work and wants something else to do, then it would be important to watch carefully for early signs that he has finished his work and prompt him at the appropriate moment to call the teacher over to inform him that he has finished.

At other times, such precise timing of prompts may not be necessary. For example, encouraging skills which are incompatible with a problem behaviour may be done at frequent, though arbitrary, intervals within the setting where the problem usually occurs. Thus, an individual might be encouraged every few minutes to use his hands in constructive activities in order to avoid head-slapping, or to occupy himself in various activities in order to avoid interfering with the activities of others.

In situations where natural triggers for problem behaviours may be difficult to identify, prompts should be used frequently so that the individual has as little time as possible to practise his inappropriate skills.

Step Three Plan results

Results must be planned so that the pay-off for appropriate skills is greater than the pay-off for the inappropriate behaviour. This requires attention to both the problem behaviour and the appropriate alternative skill.

Responding to appropriate skills

Results for appropriate skills can be planned according to the following considerations:

What is the natural pay-off for the problem behaviour?

Reinforcers can belong to one of a number of categories which include social, sensory and material. These different types of reinforcer were described in detail in Section Two. The analysis of the problem behaviour described in that section should have provided information about the results that the behaviour achieves for the individual. The analysis may have shown that just one result is achieved (for example, self-stimulation). Alternatively, it may have shown that several different results are achieved by the behaviour (for example, attention, escape and self-occupation).

Can the natural pay-off be switched from the problem behaviour to an appropriate skill?

The smaller the range of pay-offs for the problem behaviour, the easier it is to switch the pay-off from the problem behaviour to an appropriate skill. For example, if a person throws his dinner plate on to the floor as a means of getting fast access to his pudding, then, by carefully watching for an early sign that he has finished his first course, a prompt can be provided at the right moment to encourage the person to push his plate gently to one side and then immediately reinforce him with some pudding. If a child pulls other children's hair as a means of letting the teacher know that he has finished his work, then it would be necessary to watch for early signs that the child has finished, prompt him to communicate this to his teacher in a more appropriate way, then immediately reinforce him by providing him with a different activity. If an individual is disruptive or noisy in order to obtain attention from others, then it should be possible to provide him with frequent attention at times when he is not being disruptive.

Does 'arbitrary' reinforcement need to be used?

A direct switch of pay-off from one action to another is not always possible, nor does it always provide an adequate incentive for the individual to 'do the right thing'. If this is the case, then an increase in frequency of the natural reinforcer or the introduction of additional reinforcers will need to be considered. In many cases, directly switching reinforcement from the problem behaviour to appropriate skills and increasing its frequency may be a sufficient source of encouragement for the individual. For example, if a student behaves in unacceptable ways (kicking, throwing and running off) in order to attract attention, then one way of providing reinforcement would be to ensure that attention is given for any appropriate behaviours (DRO) at a much higher frequency than is currently happening for inappropriate behaviours. So, if inappropriate behaviours occur five or six times in each hour, it would be necessary to provide reinforcement for appropriate action at least twice as often, perhaps every five minutes, or even more frequently.

In other cases, it may be necessary to increase the strength of the reinforcer in order to increase the individual's motivation to perform more appropriate actions, particularly if the alternative actions are intrinsically less reinforcing than the problem behaviour. Thus, a child who spends much of the time wandering around the classroom collecting pieces of paper or fluff from the floor to 'twiddle' might find sitting doing a puzzle a less attractive option. Providing an additional incentive, in the form of social or material reinforcement for this alternative activity, could serve to increase its attraction. Needless to say, the type of 'arbitrary' reinforcer which needs to be given will depend on the individual's preferences and the strength of the reinforcement achieved by the inappropriate action.

Often, both the frequency and strength of reinforcement need to be increased. For example, if a student is being encouraged to keep his hands in his pockets because this is incompatible with face slapping, then, since keeping hands in pockets may be a less attractive option than slapping, it would need to be made more attractive by strengthening the reinforcement for this activity (for example, putting 'feely' objects in the pockets and providing frequent attention whenever he has his hands in his pockets). To increase the frequency of reinforcement, attention might need to be given every few minutes, initially, in order to overshadow reinforcement received from slapping.

Do symbolic reinforcers need to be used?

For a number of reasons it may be impractical to use arbitrary reinforcers. First, the events which are reinforcing for an individual may be inappropriate for certain settings because they seriously interfere with other activities. For example, the most effective reinforcer for an individual may be an activity such as playing a game of cards or making a cup of tea. These reinforcers can take up a lot of time and be difficult to administer without disrupting other ongoing activities. Secondly, the reinforcer may not be immediately available (for example, going to the park or cinema, having a 'rough and tumble' session with a favourite caregiver). Thirdly, it may not be practical to administer certain reinforcers on a very frequent basis. It would not be appropriate, for example, to give a child sweets or drinks every few minutes. For one thing this may be unhealthy, and for another the child may tire of the reinforcer, which would then lose its effectiveness.

The above problems can often be overcome by the use of *symbolic reinforcers* such as tokens. The reader should refer to Section One for a fuller account of symbolic reinforcers. Symbolic reinforcers have the advantage that they can be given immediately and then exchanged for primary (real) reinforcers at more convenient times. For example, if a programme requires that reinforcement be delivered every few minutes for the absence of unacceptable behaviours, and if the selected reinforcer is 'rough and tumble' play with a favourite adult, then symbolic reinforcers, in the form of tokens, could be given every few minutes. Once the individual had earned a predetermined number of tokens, these could be exchanged for a session of 'rough and tumble' play. By using tokens, the range of reinforcers which can be used to encourage a person to use his skills more frequently can be greatly extended. Thus, token programmes can be a useful way of overcoming problems associated with having to use difficult-to-administer or frequent reinforcement.

It should be noted that symbolic reinforcers have value as reinforcers only because a person *understands* that they can be exchanged for important goods or events. Most students, when introduced to tokens for the first time, need to be taught their value and the rules of exchange. This may require a formal teaching programme, as with any new skill. An example of how a simple token system might be taught in a step-by-step way is described in Table 5.1.

Table 5.1: Teaching the value of tokens (sample programme)

Aim: To earn three tokens in half-an-hour and exchange for reinforcer (sweet)

Steps:

1. Give one token. Immediately exchange it for sweet
2. Give one token. Wait 10 seconds. Exchange for sweet
3. Give two tokens, one every 10 seconds. Exchange for sweet
4. Give three tokens, one every 10 seconds. Exchange for sweet
5. Give three tokens, one every 20 seconds. Exchange for sweet
6. Give three tokens, one every 30 seconds. Exchange for sweet
7. Give three tokens, one every minute. Exchange for sweet
8. Give three tokens, one every 1½ minutes. Exchange for sweet
9. Give three tokens, one every 2 minutes. Exchange for sweet
10. Give three tokens, one every 4 minutes. Exchange for sweet
11. Give three tokens, one every 6 minutes. Exchange for sweet
12. Give three tokens, one every 10 minutes. Exchange for sweet

N.B. Timer can be used to signal when each time interval has elapsed. Time can be reset if inappropriate behaviour occurs.

Timing the reinforcement

In programmes that focus on enhancing specific skills which are of brief duration (for example, asking for help with a task), reinforcement can be provided each time the skill is performed. However, in programmes that focus on building up skills which are continuous (for example, staying on task, keeping hands in pockets, playing with toys) or focus on encouraging all skills other than the problem behaviour, a decision will need to be made about how often to reinforce the student for continuing to perform the skills. In some cases, it may be decided to use an informal schedule of reinforcement ('frequently', 'every few minutes') and rely on people to remember to keep reinforcing appropriate behaviour. Such a general increase in positive responding towards the student may be beneficial provided people remember to maintain high rates of reinforcement. In many cases, a more structured method of providing reinforcement may need to be adopted. This is particularly so when the problem behaviour itself occurs frequently or for long periods and overshadows more positive skills. For example, a person who spends long periods of time hand flapping may initially use his hands for alternative activities for only brief periods of time. In such cases a formal schedule of reinforcement may need to be used (for example, every 5 seconds) to ensure that the student receives a large amount of reinforcement for incompatible behaviours. The interval can be gradually increased as the student spends more time on these alternative activities (see Step Seven).

Similarly, when planning programmes which aim to reinforce the student for the absence of inappropriate behaviours (DRO) which occur at a high rate, then, in order to ensure that reinforcement is delivered at a higher rate than reinforcement obtained from the inappropriate behaviour, it might be important to specify a fixed time interval (for example, 10 minutes) and reinforce the student for every 10 minutes during which the inappropriate behaviour did not occur.

Responding to the problem behaviour

Differential reinforcement means ensuring that appropriate behaviours achieve a far greater pay-off than do problem behaviours. This may mean strengthening the reinforcement for appropriate skills or shifting the natural reinforcement from the

94

problem behaviour to the appropriate actions. It also means minimising reinforcement for the problem behaviour by ensuring that the anticipated pay-off does not occur. The reader should refer to Section Six for a full discussion of the techniques for responding to inappropriate behaviours.

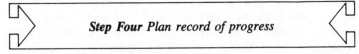

Step Four *Plan record of progress*

Monitoring change in skill usage requires the following considerations.

What to record

If specific skills are being encouraged (for example, keeping hands in pockets, sitting, asking for help), then these can be measured directly, usually by their *frequency* (the number of times they occur) or by their *duration* (the length of time they are practised) (see Section Eight).

If prompts are being used to encourage skills, it may be useful to distinguish when skills occur spontaneously and when they are prompted. Details of how prompted and unprompted skills can be distinguished during recording are described in Section Four.

If all skills other than the problem behaviour are being encouraged (DRO), a direct measure may not be feasible and an indirect measure may need to be used. For example, if a programme involves delivering tokens at fixed time intervals for the absence of inappropriate behaviours, then the number of tokens earned each day/session can be recorded.

How to record

Records of skill usage can be gathered in a number of ways, depending on the nature of the skill being monitored, its frequency, the settings in which it is being encouraged and the time and manpower resources that are available to carry out recording. A number of decisions therefore need to be made about the most appropriate method of recording.

Continuous or sample recording

If skills are being encouraged in just one setting and during a specified

95

time interval (such as mealtimes), then a continuous record may be the most appropriate method — in other words, recording each time the skill is performed during the whole session. If, on the other hand, the skill is being encouraged throughout the day, or during long periods (for example, at work), then it may be more practical to collect sample records of the skill during specific time periods. Provided that the time period is fairly representative of the day, then an accurate measure should be obtained. The length of the session can range from as little as 10 or 15 minutes for some skills (for example, staying on task) to up to an hour or more for skills which may occur less frequently (for example, asking for help with a task). Sessional recordings should be carried out at approximately the same time each day and during the same activity if accurate measures of change are to be obtained.

Type of sampling technique

The three types of sampling method are described fully in Section Eight. Selecting the most appropriate sampling technique will depend on the nature and frequency of the skill being sampled. For example, block time sampling (recording each occurrence of the skill during the whole session) is appropriate for skills which have a clear onset and clear ending and which do not occur too frequently (for example, asking for help, approaching and touching another person). Interval sampling (recording at the end of a specified time interval whether or not a skill occurred during that interval) would be appropriate for skills which are difficult to count because they occur at a very high frequency or in bouts, or because they have no clear start or finish (for example, having a conversation). Momentary time sampling (recording at specific moments in time whether or not a skill is occurring) would be appropriate for skills that occur very frequently or are continuous (for example, keeping hands in pockets, playing with toys). Figure 5.2 illustrates how different sampling techniques can be used to monitor on-task behaviour.

Continuous or intermittent sampling

Skill usage is most accurately measured if carried out regularly on a daily basis. However, when staff resources are scarce, then a regular but intermittent record will provide a fairly accurate measure of progress (for example, recording once a week or for the first week of each month). Intermittent sampling, though less accurate than a continuous record, may be more practical, particularly when programmes are expected to continue over several months.

Figure 5.2: Examples of sampling techniques for monitoring on-task behaviour

A. Block Time Sampling

What to Record *EACH TIME BEN STARTS OFF A GAME WITH ANOTHER STUDENT*
When to Record *DURING FREE PLAY (10·30 – 11·00)*
How to Record *(✓) EACH TIME A GAME IS STARTED*

Day	
Monday	✓ ✓ ✓
Tuesday	✓
Wednesday	✓ ✓
Thursday	✓ ✓ ✓ ✓ ✓
Friday	✓ ✓

B. Momentary Time Sampling

What to Record *IF ASSEMBLY SKILL IS BEING CORRECTLY EXECUTED*
When to Record *FOR 5 SECONDS EVERY ½ HOUR DURING WORKSHOP PERIODS (9·30 – 12·30)*
How to Record *✓ IF CORRECTLY EXECUTED DURING THOSE 5 SECONDS*
✗ IF INCORRECTLY EXECUTED OR IF STUDENT NOT WORKING DURING THOSE 5 SECONDS

Day	9·30	10·00	10·30	11·00	11·30	12·00	12·30
Monday	✓	✓	✗	✗	✓	✗	✓
Tuesday	✗	✓	✓	✓	✓	✗	✓
Wednesday	✓	✓	✓	✗	✓	✓	✗
Thursday	✓	✗	✓	✓	✗	✓	✓
Friday	✓	✓	✗	✓	✗	✓	✓

C. Interval Time Sampling

What to Record *WHETHER MARY INITIATED REQUEST FOR HELP*
When to Record *AT END OF EACH MORNING, AFTERNOON AND EVENING*
How to Record *✓ IF ANY REQUEST FOR HELP   ✗ IF NO REQUEST FOR HELP*

Day	Morning	Afternoon	Evening
Monday	✓	✗	✓
Tuesday	✗	✗	✗
Wednesday	✗	✓	✗
Thursday	✗	✗	✓
Friday	✗	✗	✓

Having selected a sensible and manageable recording technique, a recording form should be drawn up and a baseline measure of the skill obtained (see Section Eight). If sampling techniques are being used, then the circumstances under which baseline recordings are carried out should be consistent with the circumstances of subsequent recording (time of day, day of week, activities in progress).

How to analyse

Analysis of progress is done by comparing usage of a skill after programme implementation with usage during baseline or by looking at changes in skill usage over time. To simplify analysis of progress, data should be summarised in the form of graphs or other visual displays. These are discussed fully in Section Eight.

Measuring the effect of increased skill usage on the problem behaviour

The procedure for monitoring change in the occurrence of the problem is discussed in detail in Section Six. On the whole, recording can be simplified by recording inappropriate behaviours on the same form as the relevant skill.

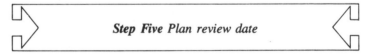

Step Five *Plan review date*

All programmes need to be regularly reviewed. A date for review should be established when setting up the programme. More complex programmes may need to be reviewed soon after starting, perhaps within a week, to ensure that there are no problems with their administration. Once running smoothly, they should continue to be reviewed regularly at no less than monthly intervals.

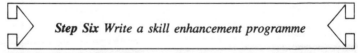

Step Six *Write a skill enhancement programme*

Whatever kind of programme has been planned — one which simply provides extra opportunities to practise skills or a complex token programme — it should be formalised into a written plan that includes the following details:

Long-term goal

This might be a statement about a reduction in the inappropriate behaviour or a positive statement outlining what the student will be doing in place of the inappropriate action (Section Three, Step One).

Short-term objective

This is a specific statement about the immediate aim of the programme. This might be an increase in the frequency of the relevant skill, a decrease in the occurrence of the problem behaviour, the number of tokens which need to be earned, or the number of opportunities which need to be made available. The short-term objective should be written in the form: *Who* will do *what* under what *circumstances* to what *degree of success* (Section Three, Section Four).

People involved

This is a statement about who is to carry out the programme. This may include information about the person who should fill in the token chart with the individual, as well as the people who are to carry out other aspects of the programme.

Time and place

The time and place where the programme is to be carried out should be stated — whether it is to occur only in certain places, during specific times, or whether it is to be implemented throughout the day (Step One).

Special materials

Special materials needed for the programme, which may include timers, token charts, tokens and specific reinforcers, should be clearly itemised.

Procedure

Instructions for carrying out the programme should include details of how to introduce the session (if appropriate), and when to use reminders to perform appropriate skills (Step Two).

Response to appropriate behaviour

Details of administering reinforcement should include information about the behaviour for which reinforcement should be given (this may be a specific action or absence of inappropriate behaviour over a specified time interval), the reinforcer itself and information about how it is to be delivered (Step Three).

Response to inappropriate behaviour (Section Six)

Recording

Details of recording strategies must be stated and recording forms should accompany the programmes (Step Four).

Review date (Step Five)

The standard form for writing programmes shown in Appendix II can be used. Examples of skill enhancement programmes are shown in Figures 5.3 and 5.4. Figure 5.3 illustrates a programme based on differential reinforcement of other behaviours. Figure 5.4 illustrates a programme based on differential reinforcement of equivalent behaviours.

Step Seven Moving on

Having achieved the first short-term objective, it is important to move on through other short-term objectives towards the long-term goal. This involves attention to settings, triggers and results, to help the student to use his skills appropriately without extra help or arbitrary reinforcement.

Settings

As the student starts to use his skills more consistently and appropriately, it is important *not* to reduce opportunities for practice but to maintain a high-quality environment which continues to provide ample opportunities for using important skills.

Triggers

As skills start to be used, prompts need to be faded, using the process of graded change, and gradually delayed to provide the student with the opportunity to use the skills spontaneously (in response to natural triggers).

Results

As the student begins to respond to natural triggers, the rules for

Figure 5.3: Example of skill enhancement programme (DRO)

Name ELAINE	Date JANUARY 2ND

Long Term Goal ELAINE WILL STOP SCREAMING KICKING AND THROWING AT HOME

Short Term Objective ELAINE WILL EARN 5 OUT OF 6 TOKENS FOR APPROPRIATE BEHAVIOUR (NO SCREAMING, KICKING OR THROWING) EVERY EVENING FOR ONE WEEK, WITH NO MORE THAN ONE INCIDENT DURING EACH ½ HOUR INTERVAL.

People Involved KEY WORKER OR NAMED SUBSTITUTE.

Time & Place 6.30 - 9.30 PM. AT HOME

Special Materials EMPTY TOKEN CHART (COPIES KEPT IN ELAINE'S FILE) ON KITCHEN WALL. STICKERS OF ELAINE'S FAVOURITE POP STAR. CHOICE OF REINFORCERS: GOING FOR WALK IN PARK. PLAYING CARDS WITH KEY WORKER. HAVING AN ICE CREAM.

Trials per Session

Procedure

AT START OF PROGRAMME TAKE ELAINE OVER TO CHART AND TELL HER SHE WILL NOW EARN TOKENS FOR 'BEING GOOD'. EXPLAIN THAT THIS MEANS NO SCREAMING, KICKING OR THROWING. ASK HER WHAT SHE WANTS AS A TREAT FOR BEING GOOD. REMIND HER THAT SHE MUST EARN 5 TO GET HER TREAT. AFTER EACH ½ HOUR TAKE HER TO THE CHART AND ASK HER IF SHE'S BEEN GOOD.
AT 9.30 WHEN THE CHART HAS BEEN COMPLETED, COUNT UP THE TOKENS WITH ELAINE AND ASK HER IF SHE HAS EARNED ENOUGH FOR HER TREAT.
IF YES — GIVE IMMEDIATELY.
IF NO — TELL HER SHE'LL NEED TO TRY HARDER TOMORROW.
IF ELAINE BEHAVES INAPPROPRIATELY DURING THE EVENING REMIND HER THAT SHE MUST BE GOOD TO EARN A TOKEN.

Response to Appropriate Behaviour

IF NOT MORE THAN ONE INAPPROPRIATE BEHAVIOUR HAS OCCURRED, PRAISE HER AND LET HER PUT A STICKER ON THE CHART.

Response to Inappropriate Behaviour

IF SHE HAS SCREAMED, KICKED OR THROWN MORE THAN ONCE, TELL HER SHE'S BEEN NAUGHTY, TELL HER WHY AND TELL HER SHE HASN'T EARNED HER TOKEN.

Generalisation

Recording MAKE A NOTE OF INAPPROPRIATE BEHAVIOURS DURING EACH ½ HOUR INTERVAL ON THE TOKEN CHART. PUT COMPLETE CHARTS IN ELAINE'S FILE

Date of Review JANUARY 16TH

Figure 5.4: Example of skill enhancement programme (DRE)

Name JIMMY	Date 3RD MAY

Long Term Goal

JIMMY WILL STOP THROWING CLASSROOM EQUIPMENT

Short Term Objective

JIMMY WILL CALL HIS TEACHER WHENEVER HE HAS FINISHED A PIECE OF WORK EACH DAY FOR 5 CONSECUTNE DAYS.

People Involved DORA AND JANE

Time & Place CLASSROOM. ALL DAY.

Special Materials NONE	Trials per Session

Procedure

DORA SHOULD KEEP AN EYE ON JIMMY WHENEVER HE IS DOING A PIECE OF WORK, TO SEE WHEN HE IS ABOUT TO FINISH.
AS SOON AS HE HAS FINISHED SHE SHOULD IMMEDIATELY SAY "TELL JANE YOU'VE FINISHED."

Response to Appropriate Behaviour

AS SOON AS JIMMY CALLS JANE SHE SHOULD IMMEDIATELY COME OVER AND TELL HIM HOW CLEVER HE IS, PRAISE THE WORK HE'S DONE AND OFFER HIM ANOTHER PIECE OF WORK, PREFERABLY SOMETHING HE ENJOYS DOING.

Response to Inappropriate Behaviour

IF JIMMY THROWS HIS WORK OR OTHER EQUIPMENT JANE SHOULD IGNORE HIM AND CONTINUE ATTENDING TO THE OTHER CHILDREN. AFTER 10 SECONDS DORA TO REPEAT THE PROMPT AND CONTINUE UNTIL JIMMY CALLS JANE OVER.

Generalisation

Recording RECORD ON ENCLOSED RECORDING FORM: 1. NUMBER OF APPROPRIATE RESPONSES. 2. NUMBER OF PROMPTS. 3. NUMBER OF INAPPROPRIATE RESPONSES.	Date of Review 24TH MAY

delivering reinforcement may need to be changed. In particular, it may be important to begin to withhold reinforcement from responses that still require a prompt, and reinforce only those that occur spontaneously so that the student learns that spontaneous performance of skills at appropriate times is required.

When arbitrary reinforcement is being delivered on a fixed time schedule (for example, every 10 minutes), it is important, as soon as the student is regularly earning reinforcement, to start to extend this time period. Thus, the student could be required to refrain from inappropriate behaviours for 15 minutes, then 20 minutes, then half an hour, in order to earn a reinforcer. As behaviour improves, the period could be extended further to 1 hour, 2 hours, half a day, all day, until arbitrary reinforcement is gradually phased out. When building up specific skills, a similar procedure could be used. Thus, a person may be required to remain at his work station for 5, 10, 15, 20 then 30 minutes before earning reinforcement. Once the long-term goal is achieved (for example, to remain at the work station for half an hour), arbitrary reinforcement could be given for two consecutive days' success, then three consecutive days, and so on, until arbitrary reinforcement is phased out. Natural social reinforcers, such as praise or attention, should continue to be given intermittently.

In order to maintain a high level of skill usage, programmes should be extended and faded out systematically and gradually, and not abandoned abruptly when the student starts to make progress. If this happens progress is unlikely to be maintained.

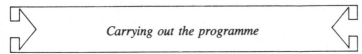

Carrying out the programme

Programmes based on the reinforcement of existing skills can be difficult to implement and to sustain. In the first place the novel aspects of a person's behaviour (new skills) or the more unusual aspects (unacceptable behaviours) are much more likely to be noticed than skills that have already been learned. In the second place the design of such programmes can sometimes be quite complex. Thus, two aspects of carrying out these programmes need further consideration: implementation and maintenance.

Implementing programmes

Introducing programmes gradually

Getting programmes under way may seem an overwhelming undertaking. To simplify this task, programmes can be started on a short, sessional basis. Once staff and student have become accustomed to the imposed structure of the session, the programme can be gradually extended by introducing a second session, then a third, and so on until the programme extends throughout the day. Introducing a programme gradually enables those setting it up to test out its practicability and make modifications which will achieve smoother running of the programme before others involved in its implementation become discouraged by unnecessary complexity. A second advantage of introducing a programme gradually is that, having established its success in one setting, it can subsequently be easier to persuade others to continue and extend the programme to other settings, since they know that the programme is a successful one.

Remembering to implement programmes

Programmes that rely on a high frequency of reinforcement for all appropriate behaviours or even for selected behaviours depend for their success on people remembering to administer reinforcement whenever it is appropriate. Providing reminders may be a useful way of helping people to remember. Reminders can be provided in several ways. They might be carried by the student themselves — for example, a special badge to remind people to take note of all positive behaviours and give frequent social reinforcement for them. They may be displayed within the daily setting — for example, colourful posters around the walls to remind people to watch for specific triggers and prompt more appropriate actions to replace anticipated problem behaviours. They may be carried by the people implementing the programmes — for example, a wrist band with a reminder written on it to keep promoting and reinforcing the use of specific incompatible skills. When formal programmes are used which rely on administering reinforcement at regular predetermined time intervals, a reminder may be needed which can signal that the time period has elapsed. Such reminders can include kitchen timers which can easily be reset when inappropriate behaviours occur, or wristwatch alarms. When using token programmes, charts can be displayed on a wall and filled in by the individual at the end of each session. This will serve as a reminder to those carrying out the programme to provide reinforcement appropriately, in addition to keeping the student informed about his progress.

Sustaining programmes

Taking a long-term perspective in behavioural management is not easy to do. Individual short-term objectives may take months to achieve. Long-term goals may take years. It is therefore essential to take all possible steps to increase the likelihood that programme initiatives will be carried through. There are no guaranteed methods but certain measures can be taken to increase the likelihood that this will happen.

Keeping working towards long-term objectives

Having established a programme and effected change in the person's behaviour, a programme should be systematically faded out by reducing the frequency of arbitrary reinforcers and triggers (Step Seven). This can be done by ensuring that programmes are regularly reviewed, short-term objectives carefully formulated and records of progress produced during reviews to help make decisions about whether a programme needs to be modified or changed. Programmes that remain unchanged over long periods of time lose their sense of urgency, and people become careless about their implementation.

Reinforcing staff efforts

Those carrying out programmes need to be reinforced for their efforts, just as the individual needs reinforcing for his or her skills. One way to do this is to maintain up-to-date visual displays of the person's progress (charts or graphs) which provide feedback to staff about the student's and, therefore, their own success.

Ensuring that all those implementing the programme understand and agree with it

This is best achieved by ensuring that programmes are drawn up with the full participation of all those involved in their implementation. This requires joint discussion and decision making and joint reviews of progress. Working in this way can be time consuming, and sometimes unanimous decisions can be hard to achieve. However, involving people in decision making and in reviewing progress increases their commitment to the success of the

105

programmes and hence increases the likelihood that efforts will be sustained over time. Working within such a framework requires a formal organisational structure which permits and supports this mode of working. Section Nine deals in greater depth with this important issue.

SUMMARY

It is a theme of this book that a long-term perspective should be taken in behaviour management. Unacceptable behaviours need to be reduced. However, unless the individual can be taught to use more acceptable alternative skills, then he is likely to find other immediately effective and inappropriate behaviours which will achieve similar results. Alternatively the same unacceptable behaviour may reappear at a later time. New skills can take a long time to learn. For this reason it is important to look closely at the individual's existing skills to see whether there are skills available which could be utilised in the management of the problem behaviour and which can be enhanced. There are a number of reasons why people may not use the skills they have learned. For one thing, they may not be given the opportunity to practise them. For another, the pay-offs from these acceptable behaviours may not be as powerful as the pay-off from behaviours which are identified as problems.

Relevant STAR factors need to be carefully assessed and the environment restructured to encourage and facilitate use of positive skills. Plans must be formalised into written programmes, and systematic recording techniques must be used to monitor progress, as in all aspects of the STAR approach. In this section we have described the general principles for enhancing existing skills and the specific steps which, if systematically followed, will help the reader plan, write and carry out programmes that use an individual's existing skills for the management of a problem behaviour.

ENHANCING EXISTING SKILLS
SUMMARY OF STEPS

1

Make available opportunities to practise skills

2

Provide triggers to elicit skills if necessary

3

Plan reinforcing results for skill usage

4

Plan records of progress

5

Set review date

6

Write programme for enhancing skills

7

Move on towards long-term goal

6

REDUCING
PROBLEM BEHAVIOURS

The theme of this book is that problem behaviours are skilled actions which are meaningful because they achieve important results for a person. There has been great stress on the fact that a long-term perspective must be taken in the management of actions and that the ultimate resolution of these problem behaviours will depend upon the learning or increased use of important alternative skills. These skills will provide the student with greater control over those aspects

Figure 6.1

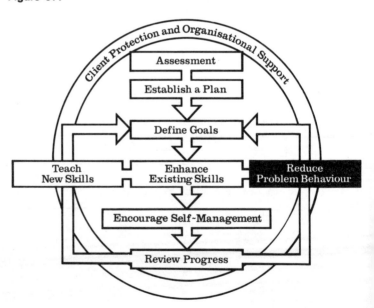

of the environment associated with the occurrence of the problem behaviour. (It is no coincidence that the sections on skill building and skill enhancement precede the present section.) However, progress in teaching useful new skills and enhancing existing skills can take a long time to achieve with people who have learning disabilities. As a result the impact of such interventions upon the problem behaviours may not be immediate. In the case of serious behaviour problems it therefore becomes necessary to find ways of effecting a more immediate reduction in the problem behaviour while new skills are being learned and existing skills are being strengthened.

A. GENERAL PRINCIPLES FOR REDUCING PROBLEM BEHAVIOURS

There are many methods for reducing behaviour problems in the short term. These methods are based upon the assessment and manipulation of the same STAR factors which have been discussed throughout this book. Just like any skill, most actions which are defined as problematic or unacceptable occur within specific setting conditions. They may be triggered by specific events and gain observable and significant results for the person. A careful assessment and analysis of these STAR factors (see Section Two) will suggest which of these STAR factors might be most effectively altered with least distress to the student.

Altering settings

Interventions at this level vary in complexity and time requirements. Nevertheless they need to be incorporated into a plan for dealing with a problem behaviour, since it is most unlikely that specific programmes to alter triggers and results can be effective if underlying setting conditions are not altered as well. Thus attention needs to be paid to 'atmosphere' factors which may be affecting the individual (for example, conflict between parents, tensions arising from staff leaving a residential unit). 'State' factors, too, (for example, pain, tiredness, depression) will need to be treated if they influence the occurrence of problem behaviours.

Other more general setting conditions, such as waiting times and lack of occupation, which predispose the individual to behaving inappropriately, may need to be attended to. Some of these situations may be resolved by teaching the individual new skills and encouraging him to practise existing skills. But these are longer term goals which will take time to achieve. In the more immediate term many of these situations can be avoided by cutting down unnecessary rules (for example, no-one can leave the table until everyone has finished; everyone must be sitting down before anyone can eat). Many people with these problems are cared for in groups which vary widely in their needs and where the pace is set by those whose needs are greatest. It is important to recognise that these times provide potential setting conditions for behaviour difficulties, and to plan accordingly.

Setting factors which relate to problem behaviours are many and varied. Intervening to change these factors can sometimes be straightforward, but sometimes it can be complex. Some of the methods of intervention are beyond the scope of this book. Nevertheless, it is important to be aware of these factors and to be actively seeking them out since intervention at this level can effect very wide-ranging changes in behaviour and economise on the effort put into highly specific programmes.

Altering triggers

The assessment will have highlighted whether there are any identifiable triggers for the problem behaviour, that is, whether it occurs selectively in the presence of those triggers but not in their absence. If specific triggers can be pinpointed, then measures can be taken to remove or otherwise alter the value of these triggers thereby avoiding problem behaviours occurring. For example, if a specific person 'sets off' unacceptable actions, it may be possible to ensure that that person is kept away at important times. This, clearly, is a short-term solution and may create unnecessary restriction on life. A longer term solution might be to change the value of the trigger — to eliminate its function as a trigger for the problem behaviour, rather than eliminate the trigger itself. This can be done by removing the trigger and then gradually reintroducing it into the environment, in a step-by-step manner, using the principle of graded change. Alternatively, the trigger value can be changed if the result of an action previously associated with the trigger no longer occurs and some other result occurs in its place (in the above example this would occur if the person who 'sets off' the problem behaviour did not cuddle the student when he screamed but ignored that behaviour while responding to other, positive behaviours).

Altering results

The assessment may also have highlighted which results the problem behaviour achieves for the individual. If behaviour can be built up because it achieves significant results, then it can also be brought down by altering its results. There are many ways in which results achieved by unacceptable action can be altered. One way is to prevent the desired result ever occurring after the behaviour. However, although this can be a powerful way of reducing unacceptable behaviours, this procedure, called *extinction*, takes time and the first effect will be to increase the problem as the individual works harder to get back the favoured result. After this, if the result is still not achieved, then the behaviour will gradually decline. In order to be effective it is essential that the looked-for result is *never* achieved, otherwise the behaviour will continue to be performed.

A more rapid way of altering results is to prevent the desired result occurring and to add in some type of cost result. Cost results are those which, when they follow a behaviour, make that behaviour less likely to occur in the future. Individuals vary in what they find 'costly' in the same way that they vary in what they find 'encouraging'. Thus there can be *social costs*: an angry telling off, withdrawal of attention and being ignored, being excluded from a social group, having to apologise, being stared at from a close range. There can be *sensory costs*: physical punishment, physical restraint, having the television or stereo switched off, tasting something unpleasant (as in the use of bitter aloes to cure nail biting). There can also be *material costs*: loss of pocket money or tokens (see Section Five), or loss of food (as in being sent from the dinner table).

There are a number of specific cost procedures which combine two or more of these elements and which, when applied consistently and immediately following an unacceptable action, have proved very effective in decreasing the problem behaviours of some individuals. The most frequently used procedures are described below.

Time-out

This procedure involves removing any opportunity of obtaining re-inforcement within a particular setting for a brief period of time. This may be effected by removing the individual from the situation following performance of an inappropriate behaviour or by removing the potentially reinforcing event itself.

Correction and over-correction

Correction means having to restore the situation to its original state following the occurrence of a problem behaviour (for example, clearing up the mess if a meal has been tipped on to the floor). Over-correction combines correction with positive practice of behaviours appropriate to the situation where the problem behaviour occurred. For example, the student who has thrown his food on to the floor would be required to clean this up (restitution) and then collect up all the plates and cutlery, wash them and clean down the tables (positive practice).

Facial screening

This procedure involves screening the eyes with a hand, a bib, or a larger screen for a brief period of time following the inappropriate action.

Token cost

This procedure is used as part of a token programme. It involves removing tokens each time an appropriate action occurs. This therefore reduces the individual's 'buying' power as a result of behaving inappropriately.

When selecting an appropriate procedure to use, it is essential to consider which procedures are ethically acceptable (see Section Nine). Note that physical punishments are specifically forbidden in most settings. It is then necessary to find a technique that is appropriate for the individual. Not all techniques work with all individuals and techniques that act as costs for some people may be positive incentives for others. Some people enjoy being on their own; if they are socially isolated following an inappropriate action, this may encourage them to repeat the action in the future. For an individual who enjoys physical contact and rough and tumble, physical restraint may not be an effective cost. Thus a cost that is meaningful to the individual and that will effectively communicate the unacceptability of an action must be found. If there is range of suitable procedures, then the least aversive should be chosen first. Any technique that requires a lot of physical compulsion or excessive struggling should be avoided unless sufficient resources are available to handle such physical confrontations safely. In most cases it should be possible to find a technique that does not require major physical involvement. Finally, it is important to note that there is no single most effective cost procedure for a given problem behaviour. Any one of a number of procedures may be effective in reducing an unacceptable action. The important thing is to match the procedure to the individual and to apply it consistently and immediately.

When working to reduce the problem behaviours of people with severe learning disabilities, it is important to bear in mind that behaviours do not exist in isolation from each other. Sometimes a change in one behaviour will be accompanied by changes in other behaviours, often unanticipated changes. These can be beneficial side effects, as in the case where stopping somebody punching themself leads to increases in smiling, talking and approaches to others. There can, however, be negative side effects. Stopping somebody punching themself can lead to increases in head banging against objects. It is difficult to predict whether such side effects will occur. Picking up the changes if they occur will help to understand better the meaning of the behaviours and how they are organised. It may also help one to step in quickly to deal with any negative side effects.

Implementing and sustaining programmes

Planning a response to a problem behaviour in the way described above, based on a rational and objective assessment of the behaviour, the person and his environment, is one thing. Implementing such a programme may be quite another, particularly if the behaviour presents a danger to others or to the individual, or is highly disruptive or obnoxious. Such actions give rise to enormous emotional reactions in people who witness or are victims of them. The reactions can include anger, fear or general anxiety. When this happens it can be difficult to respond objectively. An instinctive response may be to retaliate — to find a 'punishment to fit the crime' — rather than to respond in a way which is part of a planned programme. For this reason it is essential to take steps to minimise the tensions that can occur, to prepare caregivers thoroughly to enable them to respond objectively, and to promote support for staff who may be the victims of such actions and who are exposed to potentially harmful situations on a day-to-day basis.

This completes the general overview of the principles involved in reducing problem behaviours. In the second part of this section the specific steps required for constructing effective interventions to change these behaviours will be detailed.

B. DEVELOPING PROGRAMMES FOR REDUCING PROBLEM BEHAVIOURS

The assessment process may have highlighted a number of STAR factors which are relevant to the occurrence of the problem behaviour, and long-term goals will have been established aimed at reducing or eliminating that behaviour. From these, more immediate goals may have been set. It is now necessary to plan programmes of intervention which will achieve these goals with the least distress to the individual.

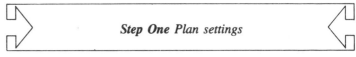

Step One Plan settings

The first step in the plan is to effect changes in setting conditions so that problem settings do not arise. Such changes can be effected in a number of ways.

Avoiding settings for problem behaviour

It may be possible in the short term to deal with a problem behaviour by simply avoiding the setting conditions associated with it. If tantrums only occur in large supermarkets, then one could avoid taking the student to such places. If aggression only occurs towards smaller children or very dependent people, then the student could be kept away from settings where such people are present.

It may be possible to retain the individual within existing settings but alter these in such a way as to eliminate those aspects of the setting related to the problem behaviour. For example, if furniture throwing is associated with periods when no other activities are available, then making available materials or scheduling activities in these settings may avoid the problem behaviour. If screaming occurs during waiting times (for meals or buses) then either routines can be reorganised to avoid excessive waiting or alternative activities can be provided during these times.

Altering settings for problem behaviours

Some setting conditions cannot simply be avoided. They require a more sustained approach to alter the nature of such conditions. If 'state' variables such as loss of sleep in the night is associated with tantrums the following day, then a programme to improve overall sleep patterns may help deal with daytime tantrums. If depressed mood is the setting for problem behaviours, then treatment for the depression will be needed. Such interventions may take considerable time to have any effect. This is also true in relation to 'atmosphere' variables such as tension between parents or conflict among staff. These can be resolved if a staff or family group is given sustained help by an outside agent to uncover and analyse their difficulties and find ways of resolving them.

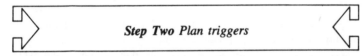

Step Two Plan triggers

There are a number of possible ways of manipulating triggers of problem behaviour. Selection of a strategy will depend on the nature of the trigger itself and the practicability of the various types of intervention.

Avoiding triggers for problem behaviours

One way of controlling a behaviour in the short term is to remove the factors that trigger it. If a student in a class or workshop setting has outbursts whenever visitors enter the room, then visitors might be banned or times of visiting restricted in a way that will avoid disruption. If meals are thrown every time cabbage is presented, then cabbage can be eliminated from the diet. If an individual is 'set off' by one particular person, then changing seating arrangements or group composition is one way of dealing with the problem.

Directly altering the trigger value

The value of a trigger can be altered by changing the results previously associated with it. This is more fully discussed in Step Three, but one example will clarify this approach. If a person has learned that when a demand is made (trigger), head banging (action) is followed

115

by removal of the demand (result), then these associations can be changed in two ways. First, one would refuse to remove the demand when head banging occurs and, secondly, one would give a very large, powerful reinforcer when compliance with the demand occurred. This alters the signal value of the trigger factor: a demand is now a signal that head banging achieves no useful result but compliance does. Demands will come to trigger compliance. The meaning of an event, its trigger value, can be altered by altering the results of the behaviour which it has come to trigger.

Adding triggers for competing behaviours

It may be possible to avoid triggering a problem behaviour if other behaviours can be triggered to compete with it. The attachment of some students to routines has already been mentioned, and a break in routine or a change in a sequence can trigger problem behaviours. One way of avoiding this is to provide adequate warning about what is to happen next. Such warnings help to make the world predictable and inform the individual about which behaviours will be appropriate. Warnings can be given verbally or through visual timetables. A similar situation arises when problem behaviours occur following denial of a demand for something. The effect of such a 'No' can be mitigated if additional information is provided — such as when the individual can have the desired item or other items that are available. Such information can be provided in words, signs or pictures. A 'No' plus explanation may trigger a range of alternative behaviours where an unexplained 'No' triggers only the problem behaviour.

Step Three Plan results

A response to the inappropriate behaviour needs to be planned such that looked-for results do not occur and, if necessary, performance of the inappropriate action incurs a 'cost' result for the individual.

Removing looked-for results

This procedure, called extinction, can be carried out in a number of ways, depending on the results which are being achieved by the problem behaviour. If these are *social results*, then they will be

116

prevented by making no social response to the problem behaviour, by responding as if the action had not occurred at all. Examples of the use of extinction might be: not responding to a student when screaming occurs in order to attract attention; not comforting or pacifying a student who head bangs for attention; not flinching when a student pinches or bites in order to see a pained response; not leaving the table to clear up a meal which has been tipped in order to see the ensuing commotion.

If the problem behaviour achieves *sensory results*, extinction will entail eliminating these results in some way. For example, if an individual spits in order to play with or watch the saliva, immediately wiping away the saliva each time spitting occurs removes the desired result. If a person head bangs against reverberating objects because of the noise effect, placing a cushion between head and surface will cut out the noise result. The sound result of screaming can be cut out by providing earphones attached to a radio or cassette.

Material results may also be controlling a problem behaviour. If lying down and screaming in the middle of a supermarket 'produces' crisps or sweets, then these will have to be withheld when such tantrums occur; likewise if head banging is comforted by tea and biscuits.

Not all the results achieved by problem behaviours are positive gains. Equally powerful in maintaining a behaviour are results which lead to *escape from a negative situation* (for example, from task demands or social interaction). In these cases extinction means preventing such escape. If a student hand bites whenever asked to wash or dress with the result that these activities are done for him, then preventing escape means insisting that the activities are carried out despite the hand biting. If a student has a temper tantrum when asked to work at a table activity and this results in his being allowed to leave the activity, then escape will be prevented if activity completion is insisted upon despite the outburst. A student might head bang whenever approached by a member of staff and this results in the staff withdrawing. Preventing escape means continuing with the interaction despite the head banging.

The strategy of extinction can be very powerful in decreasing problem behaviours. It is, however, essential that preventing escape or withholding positive results occurs every single time that the problem behaviour occurs — otherwise the behaviour will be reinforced intermittently and this will make it very resistant to extinction. It is also important to remember that when anticipated results are not forthcoming the student will try harder to gain these results. In the first instance the problem behaviour will increase in frequency and/or become more intense. If such an escalation in behaviour is not manageable or acceptable — as in some cases of severe self-injury, aggression or destructiveness — then other procedures which will more rapidly decrease the behaviour will have to be considered.

Applying cost results

When selecting a cost procedure, it is important to select one which is practicable to implement and which will successfully communicate the unacceptability of the problem behaviour to the individual.

Time-out

This might include a number of specific procedures. Thus withdrawal of attention — turning away, ceasing all interaction — might be one means of time-out. Another might be withdrawing the individual from a situation — sending him to a chair in the corner of the room, putting him outside in the corridor, sending him to a bedroom or sending him to a designated time-out room which is free of any potentially reinforcing stimuli. A third means of time-out is the converse of withdrawing the individual who behaves inappropriately: other people withdraw themselves, for example, by walking out of the room every time a temper outburst occurs. There are also symbolic ways of effecting time-out. An individual might wear a badge as long as his behaviour remains appropriate. If inappropriate behaviour occurs the badge can be removed. The people working with the individual would only interact with him when the badge was on, and likewise favourite activities could only be permitted when the badge was on. Finally, it should be remembered that people are not the only reinforcing events in the environment. Other things act as reinforcers and access to these can be withdrawn following a problem behaviour (for example, removing a personal stereo or switching off the television each time a person starts to rock or hand flap).

When using time-out the following rules should be observed:

(a) Time-out should be brief (no more than 10 minutes, and preferably 2–5 minutes). Longer periods may exceptionally be used but only after careful consideration (see Section Nine).
(b) The time-out period to be used must be specified in advance and not left to individual discretion.
(c) The individual must be kept under observation during time-out.

(d) Time-out should end once the predetermined interval has elapsed.

(e) If the individual is still behaving inappropriately at the end of the specified interval, time-out should be extended until he has remained acting appropriately for at least 5 seconds. Otherwise the student may learn that inappropriate behaviour leads to release from time-out (escape learning).

Correction and over-correction

Correction — having to restore a situation to its original state following the occurrence of a problem behaviour — can encompass a variety of actions. Thus, a student might be required to wipe down a table which has been spat upon, wash himself and his clothing if wet and/or soiled, pick up furniture which has been tipped over. The important thing is that the student makes the effort to restore the situation. Over-correction — which combines restitution with positive practice — may also encompass a range of procedures. For example, a student who tips furniture might be required to pick up all the furniture (restitution) and then tidy and polish all other furniture in the room (positive practice). Restitution and positive practice can be used separately. Correction is just restitution. An example of the use of positive practice occurs with the person who engages in self-stimulatory hand flapping. This does not disturb anything in the environment so restitution is not appropriate. Positive practice would involve the individual engaging in a series of appropriate hand movements (hands folded, hands in pocket, hands in lap) each time flapping occurred.

When using correction and over-correction procedures, the following rules should be observed:

(a) Correction and over-correction should be brief (usually no more than 5 minutes and preferably 1 or 2 minutes).

(b) Although some physical prompting may be necessary to ensure compliance with instructions, there should not be major physical confrontations. Continued serious physical resistance would indicate the need to use an alternative procedure.

(c) No reinforcement should be given at any time during correction and over-correction procedures.

Restraint

Physical restraint can be implemented in a number of ways. It may involve the whole body (lying a student flat on the floor, or sitting a student on the floor with his head between his knees) or it may involve part of the body (holding a student's hands by his sides). As with all cost procedures, stringent rules for using restraint should be observed:

(a) Restraint should be as brief as possible (as little as 5 or 10 seconds may be sufficient); but
(b) Release from restraint should depend upon the student not struggling, and remaining calm for at least 5 seconds;
(c) Because of the dangers of some restraint procedures to both staff and students, the procedures should be practised in role play to ensure that the method is safe and easy to implement.

Facial screening

When using this procedure the following rules should be observed:

(a) Screening should be applied for 10–60 seconds, but
(b) The screen should be removed only if the individual has not struggled for at least 5 seconds;
(c) Continual serious physical resistance beyond the first week of the programme would indicate the need to shift to an alternative procedure.

Token cost

Token cost procedures, which are part of a token programme, can be implemented in two ways. The individual can earn tokens for specific positive behaviours and lose these when problems occur. Alternatively, the individual can be provided with a set number of tokens at the start of a session. A fixed number would then be removed each time the problem behaviour(s) occurred. A token programme must specify the period of time over which earning takes place, the times at which tokens can be exchanged for back-up reinforcers and the maximum number of tokens that can be earned. The number of tokens that must be earned in order to exchange for back-up reinforcers should also be specified. There might be a single back-up reinforcer at a fixed price: the individual either earns it or not. More sensitively, there can be a range of back-up reinforcers with different prices, the most powerful reinforcers having the highest price.

When using token costs the following rules should be observed:

(a) The student must have some understanding of token values (see Section Five).
(b) It should be easy for the student to earn or retain more tokens than are likely to be lost.
(c) Exchange of tokens for reinforcers should occur immediately after a session at a predetermined time.
(d) Tokens should be removed immediately following inappropriate actions.

General rules for applying cost procedures

Having selected a cost procedure suitable for the individual, it is then a question of applying it in the way most likely to achieve a change in behaviour. This means:

(a) The procedure must be implemented *immediately* following the problem behaviour (or, even better, as the behaviour starts).
(b) The procedure must be implemented *every time* that the problem occurs.
(c) If instructions have to be used, they should be brief and given once only.
(d) In most cases, immediately before implementing a cost procedure, the student's name should be called followed by 'No' spoken in a sharp voice. This will build up an association between 'No' and a cost result, so that 'No' becomes a powerful warning signal, which will come to trigger the stopping of a problem behaviour (to escape from the cost procedure).

It may be necessary to try out a number of procedures before a practicable and effective one is found. In order to judge the effectiveness of a procedure a concise record of the individual's behaviour will need to be kept so that decisions about programme continuation or change can be based on the objective information.

***Step Four** Plan record of progress*

There are a number of ways of gathering records of a problem behaviour. Thus, a planned choice needs to be made.

Continuous or sessional recording

Continuous recording provides the most accurate measure of change but sessional recording can be quite accurate if a 'typical' time period is selected. If a student rarely hits other people during unstructured times, it would be pointless to select these times for observation. It would be better to select a more representative time — perhaps one hour out of the morning's structured activity.

Complete or sample measures

The second decision is whether to keep a record of every occurrence of the behaviour or whether to take a sample measure of the behaviour. Obviously a record of every occurrence is the most accurate measure, but it can be very time consuming and difficult to carry out in practical situations. This is particularly true when the behaviour occurs very frequently. If it is not possible to keep complete records, then either momentary, time or interval sampling (see Section Eight) can be used. The more frequent the sampling, the more accurate the measure. The following can be used as a rough guide for selecting a recording system:

Complete recording. If the behaviour occurs no more than once every 15–30 minutes or occurs in long bouts (such as screaming) separated by at least this amount of time.

Momentary time sampling. If the behaviour is continuous or occurring with very short time periods in-between occurrences (for example, some kind of stereotyped behaviour such as hand flapping).

Interval sampling. If the behaviour occurs moderately frequently and lasts only a short time when it does occur or occurs in long bouts.

One can choose any combination of these record systems. Selection of a system will depend on the frequency of the behaviour and the resources available for recording. Figure 6.2 provides an illustration of how different recording systems would represent the occurrence of hair pulling over a 12-hour period.

Having selected a recording system for monitoring change in the problem behaviour, it is important to prepare a recording sheet and then take a baseline measure of the behaviour before implementing any programme of change (see Section Eight).

Figure 6.2: Examples of sampling techniques for monitoring problem behaviours

A. Total Record

What to record	HAIR PULLING
When to record	THROUGHOUT DAY WHENEVER SAM PULLS PEOPLE'S HAIR
How to record	NOTE TIME, PLACE, PERSON

Date	Hair Pulling	
12TH APRIL	8·10 PULLED A'S HAIR IN BATHROOM	
	8·30 PULLED J'S HAIR AT BREAKFAST	
	8·54 PULLED A'S HAIR ON BUS	
	9·37 PULLED D'S HAIR IN CLASS	
	9·40 PULLED D'S HAIR AGAIN IN SWIMMING	
	10·56 PULLED S'S HAIR IN SOFT PLAY	
	11·20 PULLED T'S HAIR WAITING FOR DRIVER	
	12·30 PULLED D'S HAIR IN PLAYGROUND	
	12·37 PULLED S'S HAIR IN PLAYGROUND	
	12·50 PULLED T'S HAIR IN PLAYGROUND	
	TOTAL FREQUENCY	10

B. Interval Time Sampling

| What to record |
| HAIR PULLING |

| When to record |
| EVERY ½ HOUR FOR BEHAVIOUR DURING PREVIOUS ½ HOUR. |

| How to record |
| ✓ IF PULLED HAIR |
| ✗ IF DIDN'T PULL HAIR |

Date	Interval	✓/✗
12TH APRIL	7·00 - 7·30	✗
	7·30 - 8·00	✗
	8·00 - 8·30	✓
	8·30 - 9·00	✓
	9·00 - 9·30	✗
	9·30 - 10·00	✓
	10·00 - 10·30	✗
	10·30 - 11·00	✓
	11·00 - 11·30	✓
	11·30 - 12·00	✗
	12·00 - 12·30	✗
	12·30 - 1·00	✓
TOTAL INTERVALS IN WHICH BEHAVIOUR OCCURRED		6 (OUT OF POSSIBLE 12)

C. Momentary Time Sampling

| What to record |
| HAIR PULLING |

| When to record |
| LAST 5 SECONDS OF EACH ½ HOUR ONLY FOR BEHAVIOUR DURING THESE 5 SECONDS. |

| How to record |
| ✓ IF PULLED HAIR |
| ✗ IF DIDN'T PULL HAIR |

Date	Time	✓/✗
12TH APRIL	7·00	✗
	7·30	✗
	8·00	✗
	8·30	✓
	9·00	✗
	9·30	✗
	10·00	✗
	10·30	✗
	11·00	✗
	11·30	✗
	12·00	✗
	12·30	✓
	1·00	✗
TOTAL TIME POINTS AT WHICH BEHAVIOUR OCCURRING		2 (OUT OF POSSIBLE 13)

123

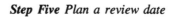

Step Five *Plan a review date*

As with all programmes a date for review must be specified at the time of planning and writing the programme. Time must be allowed for the programme to be implemented consistently, and three or four weeks is a reasonable period for a review of this type of programme.

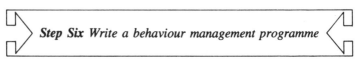

Step Six *Write a behaviour management programme*

A management programme is a written summary of the decisions made based on the analysis and plan described in the preceding steps. It should include the following details:

Long-term goal

This is a statement which relates to the reduction/elimination of the problem behaviour. (See Section Three, Step One.)

Short-term objective

This should incorporate a very precise definition of the unacceptable action which is to be decreased. It should be stated in the form *who* will do *what* under what *circumstances* to what *degree of success* (Section Three, Step Four).

People involved

People who are to carry out the programme should be named.

Time and place

The time and place where the programme is carried out must be specified.

Special materials

Any special materials (e.g. tokens, facial screen) needed for programme should be itemised.

Procedure (avoiding problem situations)

Programme instructions should include details of:

(a) Setting conditions for problem behaviours which are to be avoided, prevented or altered (Step One).
(b) Details of how to avoid or alter triggers for problem behaviours (Step Two).

124

(c) Details of triggers to be given for competing behaviours (Step Two).

(d) Details of warning to be given about cost results to follow.

Response to appropriate behaviour

Details for administering reinforcement should include information about behaviours for which reinforcement is to be given, and details of the reinforcer to be used and how it is to be delivered (Section Five, Step Three.)

Response to inappropriate behaviour

This includes information about how reinforcement for inappropriate behaviour is to be avoided, what cost results will be applied to the inappropriate behaviour and exactly how these are to be applied (instructions used, prompts given) (Step Three).

Recording

Details of behaviours to be recorded must be stated, and recording forms should accompany the programme (Step Four).

Review date (Step Five)

An example of a management programme is shown in Figure 6.3.

Step Seven Moving on

As in all types of STAR programmes, long-term goals are achieved by working through a series of short-term objectives. Once a short-term objective has been achieved, it is essential to 'move on' towards the long-term goal. This is done using the process of graded change, in other words, proceeding systematically in a step-by-step manner.

Settings

If problem behaviours have been dealt with by removing settings associated with that behaviour (for example, keeping small children away from the individual) and it is considered that this is causing unnecessary restriction for both the student and those working or living with him or that such restrictions are depriving the student of an important source of experience and learning opportunity, then the principle of graded change can be used to gradually reintroduce the student

125

Figure 6.3: Example of behaviour management programme

Name PHILIP	**Date** FEBRUARY 16TH

Long Term Goal PHILIP WILL STOP SCREAMING INAPPROPRIATELY

Short Term Objective
WHILST AT THE TRAINING CENTRE PHILIP WILL HAVE NO MORE THAN 2 EPISODES OF SCREAMING A DAY FOR 2 CONSECUTIVE WEEKS.

People Involved EVERYONE WORKING WITH PHILIP DURING THE DAY

Time & Place ALL DAY.

Special Materials 1. PHILIP'S DAILY PICTORIAL TIME-TABLE & SELECTION OF PICTURES (TO BE KEPT ON WALL IN WORKROOM) 2. SIGN ON WORKROOM DOOR ASKING PEOPLE NOT TO COME IN DURING WORK HOURS UNLESS ESSENTIAL. IF THEY NEED TO THEY SHOULD KNOCK ON DOOR & WAIT FOR SOMEONE TO COME TO THEM. 3. STOPWATCH	**Trials per Session**

Procedure

1. AT START OF EACH DAY PREPARE PICTORIAL TIMETABLE OF THE DAY ACTIVITIES WITH PHILIP AND GO THROUGH IT TWICE TO MAKE SURE HE UNDERSTANDS IT.

2. WHEN APPROACHING HIM FOR ANY REASON ALWAYS DO SO FROM THE FRONT SO THAT HE CAN CLEARLY SEE YOU COMING. IF NECESSARY, CALL HIS NAME AS YOU APPROACH, BEFORE GETTING TOO NEAR.

Response to Appropriate Behaviour WHENEVER PHILIP STARTS TO SCREAM, START STOPWATCH AND IMMEDIATELY ASK HIM TO STOP. IF IT CONTINUES FOR MORE THAN 10 SECONDS, GO IN CLOSE TO HIM TRYING TO GET HIS EYE CONTACT & HOLD HIS ARMS DOWN ON HIS SIDE AND SAY LOUDLY TO HIM " PHILIP STOP THAT AWFUL WAILING ", CONTINUE HOLDING HIS HANDS DOWN AND ADMONISHING HIM IN A LOUD VOICE UNTIL HE STOPS. (STOP STOPWATCH).

Response to Inappropriate Behaviour

FREQUENTLY BUT BRIEFLY PRAISE PHILIP FOR WORKING WELL WHENEVER HE IS NOT SCREAMING. CHAT TO HIM FREQUENTLY WHEN HE IS BEHAVING APPROPRIATELY.

Generalisation

Recording	**Date of Review**
DURATION OF EACH EPISODE OF SCREAMING	MARCH 11TH

to the conditions. This can be done by exposing him very briefly at first and then gradually building up exposure whilst preventing the problem behaviour occurring. Such an approach would need to be combined with teaching him more appropriate ways of handling the setting conditions.

Triggers

If behaviours have been controlled by removing the factors that trigger them (for example, work demands) and if this creates unnecessary restrictions for the student, then the value of the trigger need to be altered by reintroducing it very gradually into the environment, using the principle of graded change, so that it is present but does not trigger the problem behaviour. This can break the association between the trigger and the behaviour. If throwing is triggered by the presence of breakable materials and these materials have been removed altogether, they could then be reintroduced in a graded way so that they are present but the throwing response does not occur. For example, one might reintroduce one small item, well out of reach. One could move on to introducing more items and making them more readily available. Each change would be small, only moving on once the student has tolerated the previous level of exposure without any attempt to throw. If a student head bangs each time a request is made for a task and all demands have been eliminated as a way of managing the behaviour, then one very limited demand can be introduced, embedded in a relaxed context (such as talking about something else) where it is slipped in while other things are going on. Both the directness and the number of demands can then be increased very gradually.

Results

Cost or extinction procedures need to be sustained until the problem behaviour is occurring at a very low rate. By this time, it is hoped, the individual may have strengthened other skills or learned new ones. Once a decision is made to cut cost results from the overall programme, however, the behaviour should continue to be monitored so that cost procedures can be reintroduced should the problem behaviour reappear or start to increase.

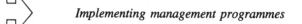

Implementing management programmes

The careful and systematic planning which is part of the STAR approach helps to ensure that successful and practical interventions will be developed. This will encourage implementation, but a number of other factors need to be considered as well if such work is to be sustained. These can be summarised under a number of headings.

Ensuring the safety of others in the environment

Some actions such as aggressive or destructive behaviours can prove hazardous to those living and working with the individual. When this happens, people understandably become concerned for their own and others' safety, and tension can easily arise so that it may become difficult to carry out programmes of change. In such situations steps may need to be taken to make the environment as safe as possible for others in order that staff can become more relaxed in their interactions with the student. Such steps may include installing shatterproof glass, bolting tables, beds and chairs to the floor, providing continual supervision for the individual and even segregating the student from his peers as a way of ensuring their safety. Those working with the student may need to protect their own person by ensuring that the environment is free of potentially dangerous objects and, where necessary, that they themselves are well protected (for example, by wearing specially padded sleeves as protection against biting). An effective means of summoning help (for example, through the installation of panic buttons) may also need to be considered. It should be noted, however, that such strategies are a way of *containing* behaviour. They are not a way of *managing* behaviour: in other words, by themselves they will not lead to behaviour change. Nevertheless, in certain severe cases, they may be necessary in the early stages of a management programme.

Thoroughly practising programmes before implementing them

Although a good method of planning will ensure good programmes, it is unrealistic to expect all the fine details to be decided upon without trying out the programme first. There is nothing more discouraging for staff than to be asked to carry out a programme which is clearly impractical from the first time it is tried. If a programme states that

128

a student should pick up anything he throws but he happens to be rather tall and heavy and tends to be unco-operative, then people can find themselves in an impossible situation. This can be avoided by trying out a programme first. This should be done initially using role play (without the student), which can be enhanced further if video facilities are available to film and replay the programme. The programmes should then be practised with the student a few times before all details are finalised and the programme implemented. Such thorough preparation ensures a fully practicable programme which will encourage those who have to implement it.

Basing programme decisions upon consensus

Working with people who have serious behaviour difficulties evokes many emotional responses. These may include pity, anger, hate and despair. Often staff groups are divided in their responses to these problems, and conflicts arise between staff. Such conflicts only exacerbate the problems themselves. It is therefore important to obtain consensus agreement on programme details so that staff feel committed to the programme. This may mean compromises, but, without these, conflicts will be perpetuated and it is quite likely that some people will sabotage the programme. This will produce the inconsistency which will perpetuate and worsen the problem behaviour. Thus it is very important to achieve consensus in establishing programmes for problem behaviours. Where controversial procedures are used (particularly aversive costs), then some staff may feel quite unable to accept this and consensus will be impossible. In this situation it is important to allow people publicly to opt out of a programme and to plan around this. This is far better than insisting that everyone participate and then finding some people are refusing to implement the programme, which again produces inconsistency. Thus if consensus cannot be achieved, it is essential to be clear about who will not participate and to ensure that the programme plan is based only upon the efforts of those who are in agreement.

Ensuring adequate social support for staff

This again arises from the recognition of the responses to problem behaviours. It is also based on the fact that those dealing with such behaviours often feel isolated as they recognise many other people avoiding more difficult clients. It is important for people to feel supported in their job, for others to admire, respect and value what they are doing. It is important, too, that they can call upon practical help in order to facilitate their work (for example, relief after handling a serious incident). Such social support can be provided in a number of ways. Outsiders such as visiting professionals can help, but more important is the support that can be developed within a service system (school, day centre, youth club). It is essential to define the student's problem as the concern of the whole service, not just of the staff who deal directly with the student, and on the basis of this to mobilise formal and informal support to those staff.

Setting appropriate expectations

For people with serious long-standing behaviour difficulties, change is likely to be slow and variable. With some interventions problems may get worse before they get better. Staff must be prepared for this. If rapid, spectacular change is expected, then people will be disappointed and may abandon programmes which are succeeding in a more limited way. It is essential to orientate staff to long-term effort, to small changes and to the possibility of short-term relapse. A balance between optimism and pessimism is required which is perhaps summed up in the phrase 'cautious optimism'. Positive coping is a more appropriate model of work than complete mastery.

Publicly celebrating improvement

As with skill teaching efforts it is important to celebrate improvements publicly as they occur. It is all too easy to be overwhelmed by problems and see only the negative aspects of a student. It is vitally important to focus on successes as well as problems. A good recording system and method of data presentation will help in this, but it needs a positive effort by staff to dwell on successes in any review meeting or in less formal discussions about a student.

SUMMARY

There are many factors that need to be considered when planning programmes which intervene directly with problem behaviours, as intervention can be planned at several levels. Particular attention needs to be given to the settings which are the context in which problems occur, since changes at this level may have a significant impact on the problem behaviour. Failure to make changes at this level, moreover, may seriously hinder attempts to change behaviour using other means. At a second level, interventions might focus upon altering or removing triggers which set off problem behaviours. Finally, removing reinforcing results which may be achieved by the behaviour and/or arranging for cost results to follow the unacceptable action may produce a rapid, if short-lived and situation-specific, reduction in the problem behaviour. As in other aspects of the STAR system, it is essential that plans are formalised into written programmes and that systematic recording techniques are used to monitor progress, so programmes need to be thoroughly practised by all those who are to implement them.

In this section the general principles and procedures for intervening with problem behaviours have been described and specific steps detailed which, if followed systematically, can help the reader plan, write and implement high-quality programmes aimed at reducing problem behaviours.

REDUCING PROBLEM BEHAVIOURS
SUMMARY OF STEPS

1

Consider settings in which problem behaviours occur

2

Consider how to alter triggers for problem behaviour

3

Remove reinforcing results for problem behaviours:
add cost results

4

Plan record of progress

5

Set review date

6

Write behaviour management programme

7

Move on towards long-term goal

7

ENCOURAGING
SELF - MANAGEMENT

The information described in this section is of a more general nature than the highly specific procedures described thus far. Encouraging self-management is not a separate dimension of problem behaviour management but a principle which needs to be considered with each stage of a programme of intervention. The present section will outline the principles involved and describe some specific procedures which can be used to involve the client in the management

Figure 7.1

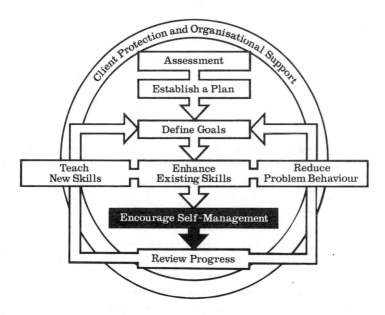

of his own programme. These procedures combine with and draw on the techniques described in previous sections.

People with severe learning disabilities have traditionally been regarded as highly dependent and incapable of taking much responsibility for their own actions. Yet as they become more integrated into the community, the demands on them to be more independent, to behave appropriately in various situations, and to take decisions and act on these, are greater than ever before. The STAR methods described thus far have focused on the efforts others must make to bring about behaviour change in people with learning problems. People other than the client (teachers, parents, caregivers or trainers) decide which skills are appropriate to build up and which problem behaviours to decrease. They provide prompts and reinforcement for appropriate behaviours, control settings, remove or alter the value of triggers for inappropriate behaviours, punish or correct inappropriate actions and monitor and evaluate the individual's progress. These methods therefore involve a very high level of external control over the individual and his actions.

Such external control can pose a number of problems both for the caregivers who implement these procedures and for the client himself. From the point of view of those carrying out programmes of behaviour change, a high level of external control can create problems for generalisation of behavioural improvements to new situations where the controlling agent is not present to provide triggers and reinforcement for appropriate behaviour or to ensure that cost results follow an inappropriate action. As a result elaborate procedures, such as those described in earlier sections, may need to be deployed to ensure that generalisation occurs. A high level of external control can also place heavy demands on staff time and effort if treatment gains are to be maintained over the long term. Indeed, there may be situations in which it may be quite difficult to implement certain aspects of behaviour change programmes (for example, using time-out procedures in the middle of a busy shopping centre, ignoring inappropriate behaviour on public transport or in the cinema).

From the point of view of the individual with learning disabilities, a high level of external control can create quite different problems. The controlling nature of the methods of behaviour change can make him a passive recipient of teaching rather than an active participant in the teaching process. Continued external control may increase dependency and impede the development of the individual's responsibility for his own behaviour, thereby perpetuating the view that people with learning impairments are unable to take responsibility for their own actions. For adolescents and adults, in particular, such imposed dependency may be quite inappropriate from both a developmental and a moral perspective. Certain individuals may actually resist such a high level of control and find ways around people's attempts to control their behaviour in an effort to maintain some control over their environment.

There are a number of reasons, therefore, why it is important to try to involve people with severe learning impairments in the management of their own behaviour, to help them take greater responsibility for their actions and to reduce the need to rely exclusively on external methods of behaviour change and control — in other words, to teach and encourage self-management.

A. SELF-MANAGEMENT — GENERAL PRINCIPLES

Self-management can be defined as a process whereby the individual directs and regulates his own behaviour by taking a deliberate course of action to increase the probability of performing a behaviour he wants to perform and decrease the likelihood of performing a behaviour he wishes to avoid. There are, broadly speaking, two levels at which a person can exert control over his own actions: cognitive and behavioural. At the *cognitive* level, he can use strategies to identify problem situations, generate possible solutions and select an appropriate course of action. He can identify his inappropriate perceptions and interpretations of his own or other people's actions and learn to modify these. At the *behavioural* level, a person can implement specific procedures which will help him achieve his goals. He can structure settings to influence the probability of specific behaviours occurring; he can manipulate cues which increase or decrease the likelihood of performing certain actions. He can provide reinforcing results for desirable actions, and he can monitor and evaluate his progress. Full self-management is likely to entail a combination of cognitive and behavioural strategies.

The acquisition of self-management skills is a developmental process by which, in the normal course of events, a young child systematically internalises the rules and norms of the adult world which are initially imposed upon him by others. In this way he comes increasingly to conform to these rules with less and less prompting from other people, by using language and thoughts to

135

mediate his actions. In addition he may learn specific behavioural strategies which help him to act on his plans and decisions. Thus self-management should not be seen as an all-or-nothing process. Rather, at different stages of development and in different situations there is likely to be at play a delicate balance between external and internal control of behaviour.

It is clear, moreover, that self-management is not a single skill. The term 'self-management' in fact encompasses a number of skills which a person can bring to bear on his own actions. As suggested earlier, these include the ability to recognise a problem, to generate possible solutions, to select an appropriate strategy, to take actions to help resolve the problem, to evaluate the success of these actions and to deal appropriately with success or failure of selected strategies. These skills are likely to have greater potential for generalisation of new learning than do techniques based on a high level of external control, because the individual can effectively manage his own behaviour, at the very least, by delivering reinforcement immediately, any time and anywhere. He can also provide triggers for his own actions in any of a number of situations.

Self-management and behaviour change

The importance of self-management techniques as a tool in problem behaviour management of adults and children of normal intellectual abilities is now widely accepted. Although the application of these techniques to people with severe learning disabilities is still very much at an experimental level, nevertheless a number of points can tentatively be made. From the available literature, it would seem that the use of cognitive strategies to mediate behaviour requires at least a moderate degree of language competence and a relatively high developmental level (3–8 years depending on the exact type of strategy and the way it is to be used). The use of behavioural self-management strategies, on the other hand, need not require high levels of language competence nor, indeed, a high developmental level. These skills can be taught using the same principles as those described earlier in this book. These are skills which, with the help of special materials, can be used by people with quite severe levels of disability. They are skills of self-recording, self-evaluation, self-cueing and self-reinforcement. Since it is these latter skills, in particular, which seem to hold the greatest promise for helping the group of people with whom this book is concerned, they will be described here in some detail.

Self-recording

Self-recording is the systematic collection of information about one's own performance. On a day-to-day basis, people rarely keep a strict count of their actions. They may be unaware, for example, how many times a day they bite their finger nails, use the phrase 'you know', or smile at their colleagues at work. However, if they wish to alter the frequency with which they perform an action, then monitoring becomes important. For one thing, keeping a count of one's behaviour provides important feedback about progress. For another, the actual act of recording the behaviour, even if recording is inaccurate, may have a reactive effect on that behaviour, such that its frequency changes.

Self-recording can thus serve two functions in problem behaviour management. In the first place, this procedure can be used as a monitoring device — the individual recording his own behaviour before, during and after an intervention programme. If self-monitoring is used for this purpose, then accuracy clearly is of major importance and the individual needs to be trained to record his behaviour accurately.

The second function of self-recording is to influence behaviour more directly. Its reactive effect makes it a potentially powerful therapeutic tool. When used for this purpose, accuracy of self-recording is less important than factors that influence its reactivity. These may be factors within the individual. Thus reactivity is likely to be greater if a person is motivated to change his behaviour. Related to this is the value that the behaviour has for the individual. If he considers the behaviour to be positive and desirable, then self-recording is likely to increase that behaviour. If the behaviour is negatively valued by the individual and considered undesirable, then self-monitoring if likely to decrease the behaviour. If the behaviour being recorded is a neutral one, then self-recording is unlikely to influence its occurrence.

Other factors which can influence the reactivity of self-recording relate to external influences on behaviour. Reactivity is more likely to occur, for example, if there are clear goals for the individual to work towards, and if he receives feedback about his progress and reinforcement for successfully increasing or reducing a target behaviour.

Self-evaluation

Self-evaluation is the action of judging how well or badly one has performed. Accurate self-evaluation can act as a strong incentive for people to alter or maintain their behaviour and is a constructive source of feedback which can give people direction for improving their performance. It is an important antecedent for self-reinforcement. More than this, during learning, positive self-evaluation is frequently paired with reinforcement, and through this association self-evaluation may itself take on reinforcing properties so that in and of itself it becomes an important source of encouragement for people in their everyday lives.

Self-cueing

This is the process by which the individual takes control of the settings or triggers for a target behaviour, thereby influencing the likelihood of the behaviour occurring. Many college students, for example, develop study skills by regulating settings in order to promote their study behaviour. They do this either by working in a library or by structuring the study environment so that distractions are reduced to a minimum (radio off, other people out of the room, desk cleared of superfluous materials). Another way by which people influence their actions is by providing specific triggers to 'set off' their appropriate behaviours. For example, people who need to arrive at work at a certain time in the morning often set their alarm clocks to wake them on time. When carrying out complex tasks, people may provide themselves with verbal or written instructions to help direct their actions in the performance of the task. Common examples of these kinds of cue are recipes or shopping lists.

In addition to restructuring settings and providing new triggers for their appropriate behaviours, people may learn to recognise existing triggers which set off their inappropriate actions and try to alter the value of these triggers by introducing competing behaviours whenever these triggers occur. To give an example, the individual might learn to clench his fists and count slowly to ten whenever he feels himself becoming angry, rather than hit out or shout at the person who made him angry.

Self-reinforcement

Self-reinforcement is a process whereby the individual provides a positive outcome for his own appropriate actions. In the course of their development most people learn to reinforce their own actions, thereby increasing the frequency of reinforcement which they receive and decreasing their reliance upon others to reinforce their actions. People on diets, for example, may reward themselves with a new wardrobe of clothes when they achieve their target weight. Working people may reward themselves for their year's hard work by treating themselves to a holiday. On a more immediate basis, they may reinforce themselves by going out to the pub or sports club in the evening after a day at work.

People with learning disabilities often remain very dependent on reinforcement provided by other people because they fail to learn to reinforce their own behaviour. Hence, the overall amount of reinforcement they receive is likely to be far less than other people receive. Failure to learn self-reinforcement techniques may occur for a number of reasons. For one thing, people with learning disabilities may not have free access to material reinforcers or activities but gain access to these only through other people. For another thing, they may never have learned to evaluate their own performance, to judge when they have done well.

Using self-management skills

Self-management is not an all-or-nothing process. For many people, behaviour is likely at most times to be under the control of both external and internal forces. Self-management skills can thus be utilised in a number of ways to help manage a person's problem behaviours or to teach him new skills. At a general level the individual can be involved, if at all possible, in planning his own programme — selecting skills to be learned and deciding which behaviours are problematic. If he is able to contribute to planning specific aspects of his programme of behaviour change (for example, selecting reinforcers), he should also be encouraged to do so. Involvement at this initial level should be seen as part of the process of encouraging self-management. Individual self-management skills may then be combined with predominantly external methods of behaviour control. Alternatively, the individual can be taught to take control over several aspects of his management. For example, when teaching people complex daily-living or leisure skills, such as road crossing, it may be possible to enhance the effectiveness of teaching by incorporating a self-evaluation component in a programme which is otherwise controlled by the trainer and to teach the individual to assess and judge his own performance during training. When teaching a person to improve his work production, teaching him to

139

monitor his own work output can significantly increase his performance rate. When teaching a person a complex sequence of actions, such as specific work skills, it is possible to help him perform such sequences independently by teaching him to use pictorial cues or to provide himself with a sequence of verbal instructions which can act as triggers for each behaviour in the sequence. To help a person manage his own problem behaviour he might be taught to discriminate and label the trigger for the behaviour, provide himself with verbal instructions to take a corrective action and finally praise himself for successfully avoiding the problem behaviour. In all the above cases, programmes could be combined with some external control in the form of reminders, feedback and reinforcement.

Self-management 'packages'

More recently a number of self-management 'packages' have been developed. These packages comprise a set of specific procedures for a number of problem situations. Two procedures in particular are worth describing in some detail since they appear to hold a lot of promise for behavioural self-management. These are correspondence training and anger management. These 'packages' contain a combination of external control and self-control methods plus a combination of cognitive and behavioural strategies for self-management. Although these packages may not be suitable for some of the people with whom this book is concerned, there are a number of individuals, nevertheless, who might certainly benefit from their usage.

Correspondence training

Correspondence training is a way of teaching people to bring their behaviour under their own control. It involves teaching people to make positive self-statements about how they intend to act in a specific problem situation, and reinforcing them for acting in a way which corresponds to their stated intention. In STAR terms, such a statement of intention comes to act as a trigger for corresponding actions and thus brings a person's behaviour under his own voluntary control. The more specific the statement of intent, the more effective it is likely to be. Such a statement may be made verbally or non-verbally (using motor responses). The elements of such a training programme include:

(a) Training the individual to state in specific terms his intention to behave appropriately in a given situation, identifying perhaps three or four key behavioural components which constitute appropriate behaviour for that situation.

(b) Immediately prior to the target situation, getting the individual to state accurately how he will behave in that situation.

(c) Immediately following the event, providing specific feedback to the individual about the accuracy of the correspondence between his stated intentions and his actual behaviour.

(d) Reinforcing the individual for accurate correspondence.

As an example, an aggressive child being taught to behave appropriately during outdoor play may be helped to do so using the following correspondence procedures:

(i) During an individual session the child might be told 'Today I want you to play nicely in the playground.' The term 'playing nicely' could then be defined using three or four behavioural statements: 'Playing nicely means staying near the bigger children, riding your bike without crashing into other children, playing ball on your own or with other children, walking around on your own.' The child would then be prompted to repeat the intention of playing nicely and the specific behavioural statements which accompany it, until he has learned it.

(ii) Prior to playtime, the child would be asked how he will behave in the playground and prompted to repeat the behavioural statement which he has learned.

(iii) Immediately after play, he would be given very specific feedback about the correspondence of this actual behaviour with his previously stated intention. 'You said you would play nicely in the playground today and you did. You stayed with the bigger children, you played ball and rode your bike without crashing into other children and you walked around nicely on your own.'

(iv) Reinforcement would be delivered according to the accuracy of the correspondence between his verbal statement and his actions. If the individual is unable to verbalise his intentions, then he could be taught to demonstrate each behavioural component of his stated intention.

Anger management

This set of procedures is designed to help people manage their anger. An anger response is determined by four factors: an external event, a cognitive appraisal of that event, a physiological response to the event (including responses such as muscle tension and increased heart rate) and a behavioural response to these internal processes (shouting, loss of temper, aggression). Self-control techniques for anger management aim to alter the cognitive and physiological response to an anger-arousing event. They include:

(a) teaching a person to recognise and label when he has become angry;
(b) teaching a person to use recognition of his own anger as a trigger for (i) identifying the cognition which made him angry and replacing that cognition with a more adaptive one, (ii) counteracting the physiological response to anger through the use of relaxation.

Techniques for relaxation training and cognitive appraisal of anger-arousing situations are described below.

Relaxation. Anger is often accompanied by muscular tension. One important element of self-control is therefore to counteract this response. Some individuals may be able to learn progressive muscular relaxation through specific training. Such training involves teaching the individual to identify the major muscle groups in his body: arms (biceps, forearm muscles), legs (calf muscles, thigh muscles), face muscles (eyes, nose, cheeks, jaw); neck, shoulder, chest and stomach muscles.

At the start of training the person is taught to tense and relax each muscle group, so that he can recognise the difference between tension and relaxation. Once he can do this, tensing the muscles is omitted from training so that he now simply relaxes each muscle in turn. Muscles are then grouped so that he relaxes two or three muscles together (left arm, right arm, face, neck, chest and shoulders, stomach, left leg, right leg). Progressively he learns to relax more muscles together (both arms, face and neck, torso, legs). Finally, he should be able to relax the whole body quite quickly. Relaxation is combined with teaching the individual to control his breathing, and a cue word is repeated during relaxation ('Be calm', 'Relax') so that it can eventually become a trigger for muscle relaxation.

Muscular relaxation takes a long time to learn and needs to be practised regularly. Not all people who have severe learning and behavioural difficulties will succeed in learning this technique. In such cases, it may be possible to teach alternative ways of relaxing.

Some people, for example, may relax easily by sitting and listening to music, others by taking several deep breaths, still others by repeating rhymes or numbers by rote. Whichever method is adopted, a cue word should always accompany relaxation practice so that it can become a trigger for relaxation in problem situations.

Cognitive reappraisal. Through observation and interviewing of the individual and his caregivers it may be possible to identify situations which typically trigger an anger response (for example, being shouted at, being ignored, being refused something the person wants). It then becomes important to establish how the individual has interpreted such situations ('He's nasty, he hates me, he's got it in for me') and teach him more adaptive ways of appraising these problem situations ('He's too busy at the moment, I can have it later'). More adaptive ways of appraising anger-arousing situations include reducing their perceived importance ('It doesn't really matter), reappraising others' intentions ('He didn't do it on purpose'), reappraising inappropriate expectations of the situation or of oneself ('I don't always have to get things right').

Once learned, the separate elements of anger control can be combined to form a chain of responses to anger-arousing situations. Thus the person might be taught the following sequence:

(1) Recognise when he is becoming angry and label this ('I feel cross').
(2) Interrupt the response ('I must count slowly to ten').
(3) Instruct himself to relax ('Be calm, take a few deep breaths').
(4) Reappraise the situation ('He doesn't hate me, he's just a bit busy to talk to me at the moment').

The skills which, together, constitute the concept of self-management are many. Some, like self-recording, may be relatively easy to learn. Others, such as cognitive reappraisal, are more complex skills which a number of people may be unable to achieve. The differing complexity of the various skills may require a quite different approach to teaching. Having outlined some of the principles of self-management, some of the more practical aspects of training therefore need to be addressed.

B. PROCEDURES FOR TEACHING SELF-MANAGEMENT

The procedures for teaching self-management are based upon the same principles that have already been described in this book. These principles include:

(a) Careful attention to STAR factors in planning and implementing teaching. Settings need to be carefully selected for teaching. In some cases, for example, a special teaching environment may need to be used, with particular people carrying out the teaching. In other cases the natural environment may be the most appropriate teaching setting. Triggers need to be planned to elicit self-management skills. For example, physical prompting may need to be used to teach clients to use wrist counters to record their own behaviours, and demonstrations may be used to teach techniques of self-evaluation. Finally, results need to be arranged so that accurate responding is appropriately reinforced and errors are appropriately corrected. Thus, for example, a person may need to be reinforced, initially, for accurate recording or evaluation of his behaviour even though the behaviour he is recording is an inappropriate action.

(b) The use of a graded approach. This means analysing self-management skills, breaking them down into teachable steps and using part-task or whole-task teaching methods (see Section Three, Step Three) to teach new skills. The skill of self-recording, for example, comprised two separate component skills — discriminating when the target behaviour occurs, and recording that behaviour — which may need to be taught separately.

(c) Systematic record keeping. This includes written programmes and objective monitoring of progress.

Using these general principles two quite different approaches can be adopted to teaching self-management skills. The first is the error-free approach to teaching described in Section Four. This approach aims to minimise errors during learning by using a very high level of external control over the teaching situation. The second is a less controlling approach in which the student is encouraged to take a more active part in the teaching process.

Error-free learning

Error-free techniques are described in detail in Section Four, and the reader should refer to that section for a full account. In general, during error-free teaching, the teacher makes use of such prompts as are necessary to ensure that the target behaviour is performed without error. He may physically prompt the individual to mark each occurrence of a target behaviour on to a recording chart. He may instruct the individual to deliver or collect reinforcement for himself at the appropriate time. He may use arbitrary reinforcers for accurate demonstration of skill usage (for exampie, tokens). Correction of errors may involve increasing the level of prompting which is provided (for example, moving from verbal to physical prompting).

Learning through demonstration, practice and feedback

This approach to teaching is less structured than the error-free approach in that it gives the student greater autonomy in the learning situation. Teaching is conducted using modelling techniques: demonstrating to the student how to record or evaluate his behaviour, and how to provide cues and reinforcement for his actions. In role-play situations, the student then practises the techniques which have been demonstrated and the teacher provides feedback to him about the accuracy of his performance. Practice then switches to the natural environment where the student is encouraged to use the techniques to manage his behaviour. Feedback is then provided about his behaviour and his usage of self-management strategies. Such feedback must be very specific and inform the student about all aspects of his performance. ('You were very good this morning. You didn't lose your temper at all. When X made you cross, you counted to ten, and took some deep breaths and asked him to explain what he did.')

The use of special materials

Many of the self-management skills which have been described in this section — in particular self-recording, self-evaluation, self-cueing and self-reinforcement — can be acquired by individuals even though they may be unable to count or speak. They can be helped in this by the use of special materials. For example, if a person is unable to count or has difficulty using pencil and paper, an alternative means of recording his behaviour may be provided for him — a special wrist counter, stickers to place on to a chart, marbles to take from one container to another, coloured beads to thread on to a wrist band. If he is being taught to reinforce his actions, and if reinforcement is to be contingent on completing a specific number of target behaviours, materials may need to be constructed in a way which allows him to discriminate when he has achieved his target — for example, when the marble container is empty, when the coloured beads reach all the way round the wrist, when the spaces on the chart have been filled. If he has limited language skills, materials may be specially constructed to help him evaluate his own performance — for example, a photograph of the student smiling may represent a positive evaluation ('I've been good, I did well') and a photograph of him frowning may represent a negative evaluation ('I've been bad, I made a mess of it'). If he is being taught to use cues to regulate his behaviour, these too may be specially adapted. For example, a set of photographs of the student performing a series of tasks may be displayed in sequence in a scrap book.

There are a number of ways in which materials can be specially adapted to enable a person with learning disabilities to manage aspects of his own programme without continual recourse to other people for help and reminding. Imaginative and creative thinking on the part of the teacher can result in greater independence for the student.

SUMMARY

Interest in the area of self-management training for people with severe learning disabilities is a recent development, growing out of continued difficulties in achieving lasting and generalised behaviour change using traditional behaviour techniques. Such techniques require long-term and consistent application across people, time and places — no easy endeavour. In addition, changing philosophical attitudes to people with learning disabilities provide a number of other reasons why the acquisition of skills by which they can direct their own actions is an important goal to work towards.

In this section some of the principles of self-management have been outlined and methods which have been used for teaching self-management skills have been described. There is a growing body of evidence that many of the skills which are embraced by the term 'self-management' can be acquired, despite quite severe degrees of intellectual impairment, although little is as yet known about the generalisability or durability of these skills. Nevertheless these techniques offer a potentially valuable addition to more traditional approaches — if not, in some cases, a viable alternative.

When planning and selecting approaches to problem behaviour management, therefore, the teaching of self-management skills should always be considered as a possible alternative to traditional methods which rely on a high level of external control. At the very least, they should be considered as an adjunct to these more traditional approaches.

8

REVIEWING PROGRESS

The STAR approach to the management of problem behaviours stresses the importance of accurate records and objective assessment of progress in all areas of work — the teaching of new skills, the strengthening of skills already present and the reduction of inappropriate behaviour. Assessing and reviewing progress is as important to successful behaviour management as are the programmes of intervention. In previous sections the steps needed

Figure 8.1

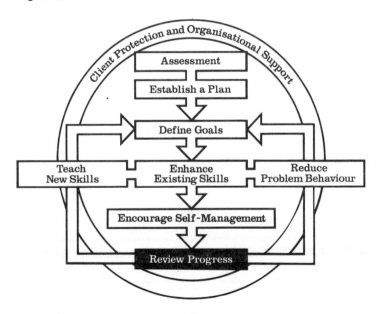

to set up systems for monitoring progress in skill learning, skill usage and problem behaviour reduction have been detailed. The present section describes in greater detail how records should be kept to ensure their accuracy and how accurate records can be used to demonstrate progress in an effective and efficient way through the use of graphs and charts.

A. GENERAL PRINCIPLES FOR REVIEWING PROGRESS

The need to summarise information

The need for systematic record keeping has been stressed throughout this book. However, the records themselves will be of little value unless they are presented in a way which is intelligible and which allows them to be easily analysed. Given the long-term perspective which has been stressed throughout this book, it is clear that records may quickly become copious and difficult to analyse unless they are condensed and summarised in a clear and concise form. A verbal or written summary or progress is likely to be cumbersome and difficult to interpret. The more information it contains, the more difficult it will be to remember that information in order to assess trends or to notice subtle changes. A far more useful and effective way to summarise information is in a visual form.

Visual summaries of information, such as graphs and charts, can be an extremely effective means of presenting information about behaviour change. They make possible the presentation of information in a way which can be grasped a single glance. In this way, they can provide a clearer, more economic and precise means of conveying information than can words or numbers. At the same time, they are interesting to look at and they hold people's attention far better than written or verbal reports. As such, they can be particularly useful during discussions of progress, such as at case conferences or reviews, where a large amount of information is being presented and needs to be assimilated by the listeners.

Because they can represent a large amount of information simultaneously, visual summaries can show relationships and trends which may not be readily apparent on individual recording sheets. They therefore provide a more comprehensive and better balanced picture than could be derived from a verbal or written presentation. Visual summaries also provide a concise and permanent record of progress which can be updated regularly without the need for summaries to be rewritten each time a new piece of information is added.

The role of accurate records in motivating those engaged in implementing programmes to persist with their efforts has been mentioned earlier. Graphs and charts can provide a visual display of achievement and progress which can serve as a permanent reminder of good work and hard effort and hence can act as a motivator for people to continue their efforts, particularly if the graphs are displayed in a prominent place and made to look colourful and attractive. Not only will they serve to encourage staff, but students themselves are likely to understand visually presented accounts of progress more easily than verbal or written accounts. If these are attractive to look at, they will be made all the more interesting to the students who may thereby also be encouraged to maintain or increase their efforts.

Organising recording to facilitate data summary

If information is to be usefully summarised in a visual form so that it can provide accurate information, it must be collected from the outset in an objective, concise and systematic fashion. Two contrasting methods of collecting information are shown in Figure 8.2. Comparing these, it becomes clear that the more lengthy, descriptive record of behaviour will prove far more difficult to summarise accurately and objectively. Descriptive accounts of behaviour are useful in the initial stages when an assessment of a behaviour is being carried out. In these circumstances, detailed accounts of settings, triggers and results, as described in Section Two, are essential. However, after the initial assessment phase, such detailed records may no longer be appropriate. During intervention, it is more important simply to measure specific behaviours which have been targeted for change and to measure changes in these behaviours in terms of their frequency, severity or duration, or changes in the amount of help needed to perform a skill.

In order to have objective records of change it is important to focus on those aspects of behaviour which are easy to measure. *Behaviours that can be seen*, such as using the toilet, putting on clothes, slapping one's face, are easy to count. If not the behaviours themselves, then *outcomes of a behaviour* can be objectively measured (for example, the amount of food eaten, injuries to staff,

Figure 8.2: General vs. specific record of behaviour

A. Descriptive record of behaviour

Date	Jim's mealtime behaviour
5TH FEBRUARY	WAS VERY GOOD TODAY. ATE ALL HIS MEAL, SPAT ONLY ONCE AND DIDN'T SCREAM VERY MUCH. STOPPED FINGER FEEDING WHEN SHOUTED AT AND USED SPOON.
6TH FEBRUARY	LUNCH. AWFUL. TIPPED EVERYONE'S PLATES AND DRINKS. KICKED ANN SEVERAL TIMES AND DIDN'T WANT TO EAT. WAS SENT OUT.
7TH FEBRUARY	SUPPER. ATE EVERYTHING BUT USED FINGERS WHENEVER I TURNED AWAY. PINCHED FOOD FROM OTHER PEOPLE'S PLATES. SCREAMED A FEW TIMES.
8TH FEBRUARY	BREAKFAST. ATE REASONABLY WELL TODAY.

B. Specific record of behaviour

Jim's mealtime behaviour

What to record: 1. AMOUNT OF FOOD EATEN (ALL, ¾, ½, ¼, 0)
2. (✓) EACH TIME HE SCREAMS, KICKS, TIPS PLATES OR DRINKS. PUT TICKS IN APPROPRIATE COLUMNS.

When to record: SUPPERTIME ONLY

Date	Amount eaten	Screaming	Kicking	Tipping plates/drinks	Comments
9TH FEB	ALL	✓✓		✓	
10TH FEB	¼	✓✓✓✓✓✓	✓✓✓✓	✓✓✓	AWFUL
11TH FEB	¾	✓✓✓✓	✓✓✓✓✓	✓✓✓	GRABBED FOOD FROM MY PLATE
12TH FEB	¾	✓✓	✓		USED SPOON WITHOUT REMINDING

weight of 'wet' laundry). Whether behaviours themselves or outcomes of behaviour are being measured, these must be precisely defined to avoid ambiguity on the part of the observer. For example, the term 'mealtime behaviour' can encompass a variety of separate actions — sitting at table, holding a knife and fork, finger feeding, taking other people's food, tipping drinks. It would be very difficult to obtain accurate measures of a behaviour which is so poorly defined since the observer would have no real idea of what to observe. To obtain accurate records each relevant behaviour would need to be defined separately or just a single key behaviour might be selected as a focus of observation (see Figure 8.2). As another example, the term 'anxious' can mean different things to different people. One person might judge a student to be anxious when he bites his finger nails, another when the student paces about the room, yet another when the student engages in a lot of ritualistic behaviour. Unless the term is precisely defined in terms of behaviours which can be seen and measured, objective and accurate records will not be obtained.

Behaviours or outcomes of behaviours which can be objectively measured can also be assigned scores. Scores can then be added or averaged and transferred to a visual summary in a way that verbal reports cannot. It is therefore important to plan recording systems carefully so that they can provide objective measures which can be transformed into simple scores.

Summarising and interpreting information

The most useful types of visual summaries of information about behaviour change are graphs and charts. There are many ways of graphing and charting information, and there is usually no 'best' type of visual summary for any type of score. Even the simplest set of scores can be depicted by more than one graphic method. Selection of a specific method of summarising information may depend on a person's preference and knowledge of the various techniques, the time available for preparation of the chart, and the particular aspect of the information which needs to be highlighted. It will also depend, to some extent, on the amount of information which needs to be represented.

If organised carefully, graphs and charts can, at a single glance, provide valuable, objective information about changes in a behaviour over weeks, months or even years. They can show

152

whether or not significant change has occurred. they can show whether there are trends in a behaviour: a gradual upward trend in the performance of a skill or, perhaps, a gradual downward trend in a problem behaviour. They can show whether a behaviour fluctuates and whether fluctuations in behaviour are systematically related to other things in the environment, such as menstruation or changes in medication. They can show whether change in one behaviour covary with changes in other behaviours (for example, whether a decrease in head banging is related to an increase in rocking or in social behaviour).

Thus, graphs and charts can be invaluable tools for interpreting information. However, it is important to be aware that their value is only as good as the quality of the information which goes into them. So, for example, a graph or chart will not show whether a particular intervention has been effective if there are no scores or measures of a behaviour before a programme was implemented to provide a *baseline* from which comparisons can be made. It may also be difficult to interpret trends or fluctuations in behaviour if records are kept sporadically and inconsistently. It is therefore important to consider how frequently behaviour can realistically be measured; whether it can be measured daily or whether an intermittent record needs to be kept. If behaviour cannot be recorded continuously, then a number of possible sampling techniques can be employed. Sampling techniques are useful because they enable accurate and systematic records to be made during brief periods of time when continuous recording is either impractical because of time or manpower constraints or impossible because of the high frequency/duration of the behaviour. An accurate record kept daily over one hour may be more useful than an inaccurate record kept over a whole day for enabling changes in behaviour to be accurately presented and interpreted. It is clear, therefore, that in order to derive the maximum benefit from graphs and charts a considerable amount of planning is needed. Such planning needs to occur before a programme is begun so that good recording systems can be organised from the outset and maintained throughout a programme of change.

There are a number of specific steps which can be taken to help organise accurate and objective records and summaries of progress. In the first part of this section, the general principles and procedures have been outlined. In the second part, the specific steps that will help the reader achieve high-quality records and data summaries will be detailed.

153

B. PRODUCING HIGH-QUALITY SUMMARIES OF PROGRESS

Having carefully defined the behaviour or outcome of behaviour in unambiguous terms, that is, in terms of behaviours which can be agreed on by everyone involved, it is then necessary to organise recording and plan how to summarise and present the information.

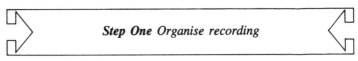

***Step One** Organise recording*

The first step is to organise recording so that objective, accurate and systematic measures can be taken. This requires a number of important decisions.

Deciding which aspect of behaviour to measure

In order to be measured objectively, behaviour or its outcome needs to be measured along a predefined scale. The most common way to measure behaviour objectively is to count its *frequency* (how often the toilet is used, how often the student kicks other people). Sometimes it may be more appropriate to measure the *duration* of a behaviour (how long the student works at an activity, how long the individual screams). Frequency and duration are the most commonly used objective scales for measuring behaviour. There are, however, a number of other objective measures which can be used. These are summarised in Table 8.1. Selecting the most appropriate measure will depend on the behaviour itself, the aim of the intervention and the level of accuracy required in the measurement procedure.

Sometimes progress cannot be measured along an obvious scale. Skill learning, for example, is measured by the amount of help required to perform the task (for example, no help, a prompt from the elbow, a full physical prompt). The tidiness of a room can be measured along a number of dimensions, such as the number of clothes left on the floor, the neatness of the bed, the amount of litter scattered around the room. In cases where an obvious scale is unavailable or would prove too complex, a subjective scale can be constructed, with each point on the scale carefully defined and a score assigned to each point. Thus, the amount of help given to perform a skill could be defined as:

Table 8.1: Some objective scales which can be used to measure behaviour change

Measure	Examples
Frequency	Hitting, placing puzzle pieces correctly
Duration	Crying, rocking, sitting, working
Latency	Time taken to fall asleep, to respond to request
Distance	Distance walked, distance ball thrown
Volume	Amount of water drunk, or urine into potty
Weight	Weight of food consumed, of 'wet' laundry
Size	Diameter of wet patch on bed, of bald patch on head

A lot of help (a full physical prompt) = 2
A little help (prompt from the elbow) = 1

The tidiness of a room could be defined as:

Very tidy (bed made, clothes put away, no litter on floor) = 1
Quite tidy (bed well made, some clothes or litter on floor) = 2
Quite untidy (bed badly made, clothes or litter on floor) = 3
Very untidy (bed unmade, clothes and litter on floor) = 4

Deciding how to monitor change

The most accurate measure will be obtained from *continuous* recording, in other words recording each time a behaviour occurs. To make recording easier to manage, however, the behaviour can be *sampled*. There are three ways of sampling behaviour in a way which makes recording easier to manage: block time sampling, momentary time sampling and interval sampling.

Block time sampling

This means setting aside a time each day and recording every occurrence of an action within this limited time period. Thus if a student has been taught in sessions to play a number of games with other children, then a record could be kept of the use of these skills for half an hour every day during free play sessions. Such time periods are likely to vary from 15 minutes to an hour a day according to the type of behaviour and the resources available.

Momentary time sampling

This means observing the individual for very brief periods of time (up to 5 seconds) but at regular predetermined times. For example, if a person spins objects at every opportunity, then observation could

155

take place for 5 seconds every 10 minutes to monitor whether the behaviour is occurring at that moment in time.

Interval sampling

This very simple procedure involves noting at the end of a specific time period whether or not the action was actually performed during that time period. No account is taken of how often or for how long the behaviour occurred. Thus, if a person has been encouraged to approach others to initiate social interaction, an observer might note at the end of each morning, afternoon and evening whether an initiation was made. Such intervals are likely to range from half an hour up to 3 hours.

Figure 8.3 provides examples of each of these forms of recording.

When recording behaviour on a sessional basis, it is important to select a 'typical' time period when the behaviour is likely to be observed. To reduce unnecessary variability in scores, the recording sessions should, as far as possible, be carried out under similar circumstances — the same time, in the same setting, during similar activities. It should be noted that momentary time and interval sampling can be used within a block time sample (for example, dividing a 2-hour observation time into 15-minute segments and recording whether or not a behaviour occurred within each segment).

Deciding how often to monitor behaviour

Behaviour should be monitored throughout a programme of intervention. Clearly a complete daily record of progress (*continuous monitoring*) will be the most accurate and provide the most up-to-date information. However, if such monitoring proves impractical, then *intermittent monitoring* can be used to obtain a reasonably accurate measure. To minimise unnecessary variability of scores, recording should, if being carried out on a sessional basis, be done under similar circumstances on each occasion. Intermittent monitoring should be carried out regularly and at predetermined times, not left to chance. An action might be measured one or two days each week, or for several consecutive days at the end of each month. It goes without saying that the more frequently monitoring is carried out, the more sensitive will be the measure of change. It is important, nevertheless, to ensure that any recording system

Figure 8.3: Block vs. momentary vs. interval time sampling

A. Block time sampling

What to record THE TIME BOB STARTS HIS WORK & TIME HE PUTS HIS WORK DOWN
When to record 11·00 — 12·00

Date	Time started work activity	Time put work down	Total time
5TH JUNE	11·00	11·03	3
	11·06	11·11	5
	11·12	11·20	8
	11·30	11·34	4
	11·40	11·50	10
	11·51	11·53	2
			32 MINS

B. Interval time sampling

What to record
IF BOB HAS WORKED AT ALL DURING EACH 5 MINUTE INTERVAL

When to record
11·00 — 12·00. AT END OF EACH INTERVAL

How to record
✓ IF WORKED. ✗ IF DIDN'T WORK

Date	Time	✓/✗
5TH JUNE	11·00 — 11·05	✓
	11·00 — 11·10	✓
	11·10 — 11·15	✓
	11·15 — 11·20	✓
	11·20 — 11·25	✗
	11·25 — 11·30	✗
	11·30 — 11·35	✓
	11·35 — 11·40	✗
	11·40 — 11·45	✓
	11·45 — 11·50	✓
	11·50 — 11·55	✓
	11·55 — 12·00	✗
	TOTAL	8/12 INTERVALS

C. Momentary time sampling

What to record
IF WORKING AT MOMENT OF RECORDING

When to record
11·00 — 12·00. AT TIMES SPECIFIED BELOW

How to record
✓ IF WORKING. ✗ IF NOT WORKING

Date	Time	✓/✗
	11·00	✓
	11·05	✗
	11·10	✓
	11·15	✓
	11·20	✓
	11·25	✗
	11·30	✓
	11·35	✗
	11·40	✓
	11·45	✓
	11·50	✓
	11·55	✗
	12·00	✗
	TOTAL TIME POINTS AT WHICH WORKED	7/12

selected is manageable given the resources available to those carrying out programmes of intervention.

Preparing a recording chart

A recording chart should always accompany a written programme. It should include the following details:

(a) the name of the individual;
(b) the long- and short-term objective;
(c) definition of the behaviour/outcome of behaviour to be measured;
(d) statement about when and how the behaviour is to be monitored;
(e) date of recording.

An example of a simple recording chart is shown in Figure 8.4.

Taking a baseline measure

Before embarking on any programme of behaviour change, it is important first to obtain a measure of that aspect of behaviour which is to be changed (for example, its frequency or duration, or the amount of help needed to perform a skill), in order to be able to compare performance once a programme of change has been introduced. It is difficult to say how many times behaviour needs to be measured before a programme is started. As a general rule, however, a baseline should continue until a stable measure is obtained which represents a true picture of the occurrence of the behaviour. So, if a behaviour occurs at approximately the same rate each session/day, then keeping baseline records for one or two weeks may be sufficient. If the frequency with which a behaviour occurs varies considerably from session to session/day to day, then baseline measures should continue until it is felt that such variability is truly representative of the occurrence of behaviour. This may require perhaps three or four weeks of observation. When measuring the amount of help a student requires to perform a skill, one or two sessions should established how much he can do independently, before introducing a programme.

Having organised recording and carried out baseline measures, a programme of change can be started with recording continuing on a systematic basis throughout the duration of the programme.

Figure 8.4: Example of behaviour recording chart

Name	TONY

Long Term Goal TONY WILL STOP THROWING OBJECTS

Short Term Goal TONY WILL NOT THROW OBJECTS IN THE CLASSROOM DURING SCHOOL.

What to Record (✓) EACH TIME TONY THROWS ANY OBJECTS ONTO THE FLOOR OR AT ANOTHER PERSON

When to Record BETWEEN 10·00 AND 10·30 EVERY MORNING

Date	Incidents of Throwing (✓)	Comments
JUNE 5TH	✓✓✓	A GOOD DAY. MARY ABSENT TODAY.
JUNE 6TH	✓✓✓✓	
JUNE 7TH	✓✓✓✓✓✓✓	ALL THESE DURING PETER'S BIRTHDAY PARTY.

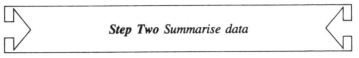

Step Two Summarise data

Two ways of summarising scores are described below.

Total scores

The simplest way to summarise the information collected is by summing measures over each session, day or week to obtain a total score, for example, the total frequency of hitting each day, the total duration of rocking each session, the total distance walked each week, the total number of times a skill was performed with no help or with some help each session.

Average (mean) scores

If the number of sessional/daily recordings becomes very large and if scores are quite evenly distributed over sessions/days, then total scores can be condensed into averages (or means). Knowing how much time, on average, a child spends rocking each day may be more meaningful than knowing the total time spent rocking each week. Means are computed by adding all the scores together and dividing the total by the number of scores. For example, to obtain a daily average frequency of hitting from records collected over seven days, the total number of hits during the whole week are added together and the total score is divided by seven. The average weekly duration of crying computed from records collected over four weeks is obtained by finding the total time spent crying during the four-week period and dividing by four. The average number of fist-to-head bangs per minute computed from records collected during a 15-minute recording session would be obtained by dividing the total number of bangs by 15.

Averaging scores can provide useful information if behaviour occurs at a fairly consistent rate during the total recording period from which the score is computed or if there is large variability in the scores. An average score may not be truly representative, however, if an unusually high or low score occurs occasionally in an otherwise consistent pattern.

Example Daily Totals of Aggressive Incidents

Mon.	Tue.	Wed.	Thur.	Fri.	Sat.	Sun.
5	7	4	6	100	5	6

The average score of 19 aggressive incidents per day in the above example does not truly represent the frequency of aggression because the unusually high number of incidents on one day has distorted the overall picture. When such inconsistency is noted in the records, then a total rather than mean score will be the most accurate way of summarising the information.

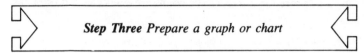

Step Three *Prepare a graph or chart*

The primary aim of presenting information visually is to represent change in the simplest, clearest and most comprehensive manner. The most common forms of visual presentation are graphs and charts.

Graphs

Graphs are an effective means of displaying trends or changes in behaviour over a period of time (for example, hours, days or weeks). A simple graph is illustrated in Figure 8.5. Units of time (session, day, week) are represented along the horizontal ($\rightarrow$) line,

Figure 8.5: A graph

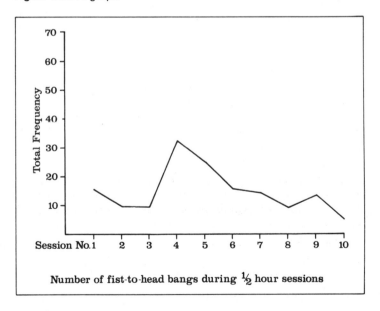

and the total/average scores per unit of time are represented along the vertical (|) line. The intervals on the vertical line should be expressed in a convenient unit of round numbers. The scale represented on the vertical line should be easy to interpret and should cover the entire range of values. A graph is prepared by indicating the total score per unit of time at a height corresponding to the total score for that unit. The points are connected with straight lines.

Histograms

A histogram can be an alternative way of summarising changes or trends in behaviour over time. It is constructed by drawing a series of adjoining columns to represent each time interval. The height of each column represents the total/average score during that time interval. At the base, the column is constructed so that its midpoint is at the midpoint of the time interval. A simple histogram is illustrated in Figure 8.6.

Figure 8.6: A histogram

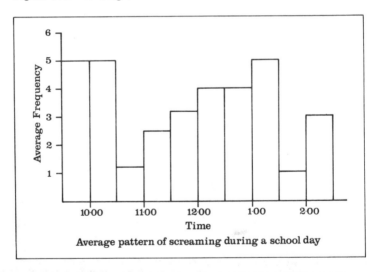

Average pattern of screaming during a school day

Bar charts

A bar chart is often used to compare information from different categories, for example, hitting versus spitting, playing with toys versus twiddling string, behaviour in class versus behaviour in the playground. It is constructed by drawing columns of equal width which are separated from each other. The space between them is half the width of the column. The height of the columns is determined by the total or average score for each category of behaviour. Figure 8.7 illustrates a simple bar chart.

Figure 8.7: A bar chart

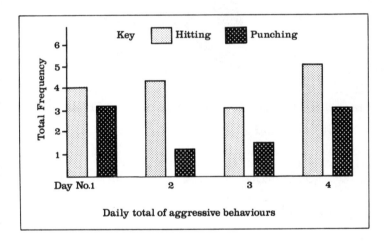

Pie charts

A pie chart can be a useful way of representing information which relates to all the parts of a complete action/event, such as a free play session or a work session. The event is represented as a circle and each part is expressed as a percentage of the whole and represented by a sector of the circle. The angle of the sector is a percentage of 360°. The pie chart in Figure 8.8 illustrates the daily work behaviour of an individual, and has been constructed from the information presented in Table 8.2 by using the following steps:

163

Figure 8.8: A pie chart

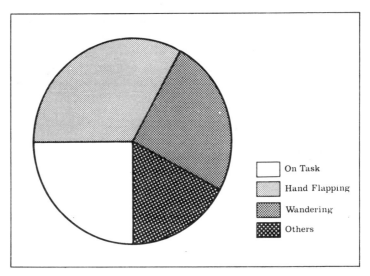

Proportion of time spent on activities during typical work session

(1) Calculating the total time spent in each activity.
(2) Representing the total time as a fraction of the total time of the session.
(3) Multiplying by 360 to obtain the angle of the sector.
(4) Drawing a pie chart using a compass and protractor.

Another way of representing this same information, using a less complicated calculation, is shown in Figure 8.9. This is done by constructing a bar chart which represents the total time of the session, and simply dividing it off according to the amount of time spent on each activity. Consecutive days' recordings can be added as in Figure 8.10 (Panel C).

Selecting an appropriate visual representation

There is no 'best' way of representing a set of data. Selection of a method will depend on a number of factors, including the total amount of information, the varieties of information which need to be shown and the particular aspect of the information which needs

Table 8.2: Calculating the angle of a sector for various behaviours occurring during a 60-minute work session

Work behaviour	Total time	Fraction of total session	Angle of sector
On task	15	15/60	15/60 × 360 = 90
Hand flapping	20	20/60	20/60 × 360 = 120
Wandering	15	15/60	15/60 × 360 = 90
Other behaviours	10	10/60	10/60 × 360 = 60

Table 8.3: Daily total time spent on various activities during 1-hour unstructured period

Day	Rocking	Walking	Playing	Interacting
Mon.	35	10	10	5
Tues.	35	5	15	5
Wed.	45	5	10	0
Thur.	30	10	15	5
Fri.	40	5	15	0
Total	185	35	65	15

Figure 8.9: Horizontal bar chart

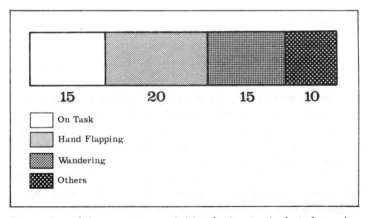

.15   20   15   10

On Task
Hand Flapping
Wandering
Others

Proportion of time spent on activities during typical work session

to be emphasised. An example can be used to illustrate how the same information can be represented in a variety of ways, none of which is more 'correct' than the others.

Example. A student's activities are observed over a 1-hour unstructured period for 5 days and the time spent on each activity is recorded daily. The daily totals are presented in Table 8.3.

As can be seen from Table 8.3, four different behaviours were recorded. Figure 8.10 illustrates some of the ways in which the information collected can be presented in a visual form.

Panel A shows the daily variability in each type of behaviour, in addition to providing an idea of the differences in frequency of the four behaviours.

Panel B shows the total duration of each of the four behaviours over the week and provides a comparison between the occurrence of the different behaviours.

Panel C shows what proportion of time is spent on each behaviour during consecutive sessions, and also gives an indication of the change over time in their performance.

Panels D, E and F show, on average, the proportion of time spent on each activity during a day.

 Step Four *Interpret graphs and charts*

In order to interpret information which has been summarised and stored in a visual form, it is important to enter all relevant information on to the graph or chart. For example, if a specific skill is being encouraged which is functionally equivalent to a problem behaviour, then storing the measures on the same graph may help determine how and if they covary: in other words, whether an increase in one behaviour is paralleled by a decrease in the other. Other items which should be entered on to graphs are significant events which might account for changes or variability in behaviour. The most obvious event is the start of the intervention. Thus, the end of the baseline and the beginning of the intervention should be clearly marked. During intervention important events such as a change of management strategy should be noted. Other events such as changes in medication, illnesses, start of menstruation, or a visit by a significant relative may also need to be marked on the graph/chart to help explain fluctuations and to help with interpretation of progress. Figure 8.11 illustrates how a lot

166

Figure 8.10: Comparison of different visual summaries of a single set of data

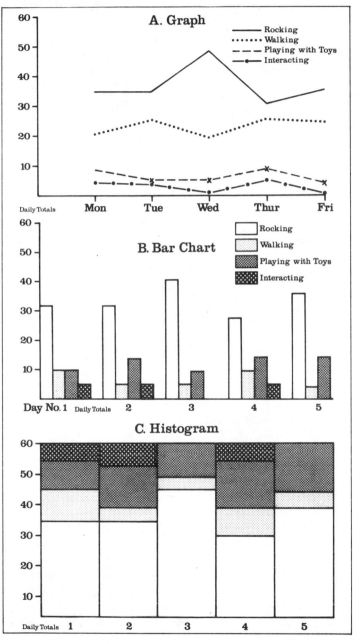

Figure 8.10: *Continued*

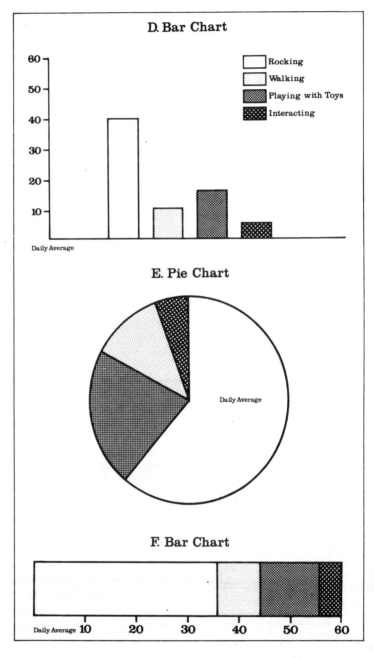

of information can be represented simultaneously on a graph in a way which facilitates interpretation of that information. The end of the baseline period is clearly entered, as are changes in management procedures. Significant events that may affect progress have also been marked.

 Maintaining good recording systems and summaries of progress

If graphs and charts are to be of maximum benefit to those making decisions about change and those who are to implement programmes, they need to be kept up to date. Information from recording sheets needs to be summed and averaged (if necessary), then transferred regularly on to a chart or graph at no less than weekly intervals. In order to ensure that this happens regularly, a few simple rules should be followed.

Appoint a named person to co-ordinate recording

A named person should be made responsible for ensuring that recording sheets are always available in the place where they are to be used and that a supply of fresh recording sheets is available in the individual's file. That same person should collect completed recording sheets regularly and file them for safe keeping until they are transferred on to the graph. Alternatively, sessional recordings may be filed after each session in a central place. At weekly intervals at least, the named person should transfer all the week's relevant information on to the graph or chart. The same named person should ensure that the graphs are brought to decision-making and information-sharing meetings for inspection. If a named person is not made responsible, particularly where several people are involved in data collection, then it is unlikely that graphs or charts will be regularly completed.

Allocate time each week for analysing data

It should never be assumed that time will somehow be found in the course of the day to fill in a chart or graph. Other more pressing activities are sure to take precedence. Graphing or charting may require up to one hour a week. (As people become more proficient at this activity, less time may be needed.) A specific time should

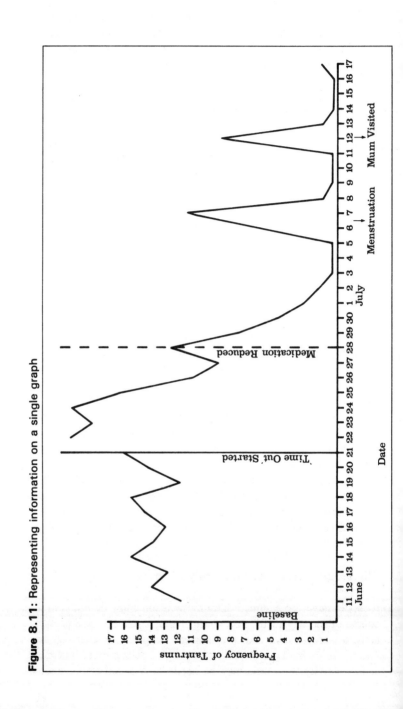

Figure 8.11: Representing information on a single graph

therefore be allocated each week to catch up with recording, to replenish supplies of recording forms, to bring charts up to date, to make a note of important events on the chart and to analyse the week's information.

Ensure appropriate materials are available

Graphing and charting cannot be done without certain basic materials. These include (a) graph paper, (b) a ruler, (c) an eraser and a pencil, (d) a supply of coloured pens. These basic materials are notorious for disappearing even in the most carefully managed settings. It is very frustrating to sit down to add a week's recording to a chart where different colours have been used to represent different behaviours only to find that the relevant coloured pens are nowhere to be found. Thus, graphing materials should be kept separately in a special place, perhaps in a large envelope in a filing cabinet. They should not be left loose in the drawer of a desk or lying around an office as part of the general office equipment.

Draw graphs and charts carefully

Graphs and charts need to be filled in accurately. This task demands precision. It is therefore wise when completing a graph, to do so first in pencil and then add colour once the accuracy of the entered data has been checked. Entries made in ink cannot be erased. When a graph contains several weeks' or months' information which may have taken someone a total of several hours to enter, inaccurate entries can prove very costly in terms of time to put them right.

SUMMARY

There are a number of graphical ways in which behaviour change can be summarised to permit analysis of a complete set of data at a single glance. Data collection needs to be carefully planned and efficiently carried out if such summaries are to be useful, however. Having done this, graphs and charts can be easy to prepare and certainly become easier with practice. Provided that information is collected systematically, graphs and charts can show changes and trends that would be difficult to notice by inspecting each recording

171

sheet or providing a verbal or written account. Used effectively, they can be an invaluable tool, not just for making decisions about programme changes and adjustments, but also for describing progress and for increasing the motivation of staff and students to persist with their efforts at change.

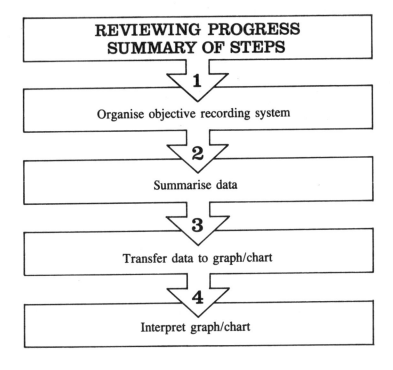

PROMOTING AND SUSTAINING HIGH-QUALITY PRACTICE

This book has described a model for understanding and working constructively with people who have severe learning disabilities and serious behavioural problems. It has been intended to help those living and working with such individuals to identify important setting, trigger and result factors which might influence the problem behaviour(s). This analysis leads directly into methods of change. These methods have been detailed, and a system for planning,

Figure 9.1

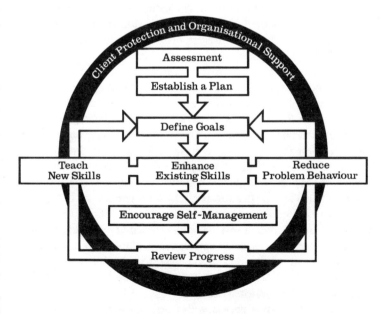

prioritising and monitoring programmes has been laid out. This system cannot be successfully implemented, however, without attention to the broader issues involved in promoting and sustaining high-quality work. These are organisational and ethical issues.

A. PRINCIPLES FOR PROMOTING AND SUSTAINING HIGH-QUALITY PRACTICE

Organisational factors

The approach described in the book makes it clear that it is the people who live and work with the disabled person who are the major influences upon that person. It is these people, rather than rare and expensive therapists, who have the greatest potential to help: it is how they behave that will determine the direction of change in the person with difficulties.

However, the amount that an individual caregiver working alone can achieve is limited by a number of factors. The behaviour of care staff is influenced by exactly the same things as the behaviour of the client. Successful work is therefore determined by the degree to which the environment offers setting conditions, triggers and results which support constructive work. This was alluded to at number of points in the text: the use of written programmes to 'trigger' carrying them out, the importance of recording and graphing as a source of encouragement for staff. It is important also to look at broader setting conditions which act to support constructive interventions.

This requires consideration of a number of other difficulties relevant to what a single individual can achieve. It has been pointed out that change in one situation (one place, one time, with one person) does not automatically carry over to any other situation. Intervention has to be carried out in all situations where behaviour change is needed. It has been stressed that significant change for a person with complex behaviour difficulties is a long-term enterprise. It requires creative, sustained and consistent effort. This is difficult to achieve working alone. Problem solving is more creative when carried out in a group context. Sustained application is more likely when there is someone with whom to share the load. Consistency across situations can only be achieved where there is adequate sharing and communication of information.

In most situations a person with learning disabilities will be in

174

contact with many caregivers, often employed by different agencies. Thus generalised behaviour change can only occur if an effective means for directing and co-ordinating the work of these many different people can be found. Some of these conditions can be created or implemented by the individual. Others require input from those at management or policy-making level. But a review of these will at least help the individual understand what is needed and 'diagnose' where the problem lies if there are difficulties in sustaining and generalising work with a person with learning disabilities. This is helpful even if it is not always possible for a member of the care team to create the necessary changes alone.

A philosophy of work

People with serious behaviour difficulties present a unique challenge to those who care for them. Often they appear actively to reject care that is offered. They elicit many, often conflicting emotions from others: pity, anger, despair. This is why people with serious behaviour difficulties are rejected from many service settings.

The sort of painstaking constructive work described in this book requires a very active commitment from carers. It means accepting that it is legitimately a part of one's job to work with such a person. Without this acceptance and commitment, sustained constructive work will not be possible. This is true not just for the individual caregiver but for the service agency as a whole. If an agency is to meet such a person's need, it must clearly accept that it is its rightful job to do so. In this book a method has been offered for interpreting severe problem behaviours which will help in this process. Rather than seeing such behaviours as bizarre symptoms of some unknown illness, it has been stressed that they should be seen as serving important functions, in particular those of communication and stimulation. They are a means whereby an individual seeks to exert some control over a world which is often frightening, incomprehensible and unresponsive. However, it is important that the agency or agencies involved with the person face these issues and accept 'ownership' of the problem as a first step in working constructively for change.

A team-work approach

The system of work described in this book is complex and time-consuming. As already mentioned, a single caregiver working in isolation is likely to have only limited success and to effect change over a relatively short time period. For long-term broad-based constructive work a team approach is essential.

Team work serves a number of purposes. It co-ordinates work within and across agencies. This is clearly essential if the consistency so much stressed in this book as important is to be attained. It is essential if generalisation of progress across personnel, places and time is to be attained: such generalisation will not happen automatically. A team approach offers access to a broader range of information, building up a more comprehensive view of the individual. Group problem solving is also more likely to be creative, generating more ideas and solutions than could a single individual working alone. Such creativity is essential when working with people who have complex needs. Finally, a team approach is also an important source of commitment and social support. Carrying out programmes requires energy and initiative, and this is enhanced by ensuring participation in decision making about programmes. Successes need to be celebrated and there needs to be encouragement to keep going when things get difficult. A team approach can offer this kind of support.

Working in teams is not always easy. There are many factors which determine whether or not a group of people work together satisfactorily. Not all of these can be covered here. But at the least the group needs to meet together on a regular basis, in a spirit of mutual respect and with a willingness to work together towards an agreed plan of action. To work effectively in the ways outlined in this text, a team also needs a very structured approach to planning and decision making. If a team is working in this way with more than one client, then the need for a highly structured approach becomes all the more important. Such structure can be provided within a system of individual programme planning.

A system of individual planning

A system of individual programme planning provides the structure within which the range of approaches to managing problem behaviours which have been described in this book can be developed and sustained long enough for meaningful change to occur. Such a system involves regular reviewing of individual needs, developing programmes to meet these needs, with such programmes in turn being subject to regular review. This system operates through regular meetings of all team members at which both the goals and the methods of programmes are planned in detail and written out. Leadership is needed and this should be provided by an individual who commands respect from group members and who has the qualities necessary to help people work together.

In order to function effectively, a system of individual planning needs to pay attention to clerical and administrative details. A system for information handling is essential. The assessment and monitoring of behaviour and the writing and recording of individual programmes will generate a considerable volume of paper-work. If this information is not to be lost, and if it is to be useful in practice, then an efficient system of storage and retrieval (paper or electronic) needs to be set up. There should be one place to which people can go to find all the necessary information on the client's achievements and needs, past and present programmes and analyses of progress.

Such a system also needs to incorporate methods of quality control, monitoring whether or not goals are achieved and whether work is being carried out in an efficient manner. If the system is used for just one person, then records of progress, such as those described in other parts of this book, provide the necessary information. If, however, individual programme planning is applied to all the clients within an agency, then further consideration may need to be given to understanding why some programmes succeed and some do not, and to deciding if time devoted to individual planning is being used efficiently. This requires a more general method of system evaluation, which needs to be carried out on a regular, scheduled basis.

Ethical factors

There is another set of issues to consider when seeking to change the behaviour of the person with disabilities. A co-ordinated and effective programme of change is not necessarily the *right* thing to do. Using an electric shock delivered through a cattle prod may stop a person injuring himself but that does not mean that this is an acceptable intervention. Praising, clapping and saying 'Good boy' may be an effective way of encouraging work skills in an adult with severe disabilities, but this does not mean that such a reinforcer is an appropriate one to use. This is the realm of ethics. A programme of change must not only be effective, it must also be acceptable.

The question of acceptability arises in a number of ways. Both the goals and the methods of programmes can be questioned. There are also many types of unacceptability. A programme may be regarded as physically assaultive if it involves, for example, inflicting pain or heavy restraint. It may be seen as a violation of human or societal rights, as in the use of physical punishment where such punishment is banned in other forms of education and correction, or in the use of restriction of movement (e.g. seclusion, time-out) where freedom of movement is regarded as a right. A programme may also be unacceptable if it adds to the burden of stigma carried by the individual. People with severe learning disabilities are often stigmatised and devalued in society and can be regarded as not fully human. The use of cattle prods and chocolate drops evokes powerful images of animal control which are severely detrimental to the long-term interests of the disabled person. This issue is linked to the 'normality' of change programmes. Acceptability may relate to the degree to which a programme is socially unusual: a judgement based upon what is 'normal' in society, what the majority regard as acceptable. This can be an important perspective from which to judge programmes.

Although there are many issues involved in the concept of 'acceptability', a very central issue is the matter of *consent*. Good quality practice is most likely to occur when the individual whose behaviour is the object of change can exert an effective degree of control over those seeking to effect the change. There needs to be a balance of control. This is a very difficult issue for people with severe learning disabilities. Such disabilities may make it very difficult for people to speak for themselves — to give their opinions and consent. Even if they can speak for themselves, they may not be listened to. People with learning disabilities have a devalued status in society which means their opinions are often discounted, especially if they conflict with the opinions of other family members or professional people. People with additional behavioural difficulties are even more vulnerable. Their behaviour elicits powerful, often conflicting, emotions in others. These emotions may trigger drastic responses, particularly in times of crisis; and control of behaviour may be achieved at the expense of gross violation of an individual's rights and wishes.

Thus it is vital to consider the multiple issues enshrined in the word 'ethics' if programmes of change are not just to be effective but also to demonstrate proper respect for the individual whose behaviour is the target of change. It is essential to give the individual an effective voice and to take active steps to protect his human rights.

There are many ways of giving the individual an effective voice to enable that person to exert control over those who seek to control him. These methods are not mutually exclusive, and each organisation will need to judge which methods are best suited to its own situation. The protection of client rights cannot, however, be left to chance and the good will of staff. High-quality programmes are only possible where there is a balance of control and the possibility of mutual influence.

B. PROCEDURES FOR PROVIDING AND SUSTAINING HIGH-QUALITY PRACTICE

A number of specific procedures can be implemented to increase the likelihood of sustaining high-quality work with people who have severe learning disabilities and to protect their interests by ensuring that programmes of behaviour change are acceptable both socially and individually.

A philosophy of work

This can be promoted in a number of ways, which will now be described.

Staff training

Any programme of staff training should include attention to the general philosophy of work. Such a philosophy needs to stress respect for the individual and to emphasise change and development as a key aim of work. Training should also include a constructive explanation of behavioural difficulties, so that these difficulties are seen as conveying important information about the client's view of the world and as being amenable to change.

Accepting 'ownership' of the problem

Before engaging in detailed work with the individual, a preliminary meeting should be organised. This should include all those directly involved with the client *and* the managers of 'front line' staff. The purpose of such a meeting is not to plan programmes but to make a public decision about whether the agency or agencies involved are committed to working through the problems (rather than excluding the client). This is why it is essential to have staff managers present. Such a public affirmation of commitment to the individual is essential to establishing the value of that individual and the work that will be undertaken. It may also be a means of 'unlocking' extra resources if these are going to be needed for effective work to be carried out.

179

A system of individual programme planning — a team approach

A system of individual planning requires a number of operational procedures if it is to work effectively.

Establishing the team

A decision needs to be made early on about team membership. It is *essential* that all those who work directly with the individual are full and equal team members. They are the people who have the greatest knowledge of the individual and the greatest influence over his behaviour. This may be quite difficult to arrange and manage, particularly when the family and several agencies are actively involved. Nevertheless, they are the core members of the team and every effort should be made to assemble them into a single working group. Their participation will ensure relevant and practical programmes. This participation in decision making is also a means of building commitment to carrying out the programme. Managers (who have access to relevant resources such as staff and equipment), therapists and other specialists with particular expertise should also be involved, and it should be decided whether this will be on a full-time, part-time or consultative basis.

Timetabling programme-planning meetings

Meetings devoted exclusively to programme planning should occur on a regular basis, not just in response to crises. Consistency is more important than absolute frequency, but it is probably advisable to meet no less frequently than monthly, i.e. meetings should occur regularly every 1–4 weeks. Length of meetings will depend upon the number of individuals being worked with, but should be determined in advance. It is probably not advisable to schedule more than two hours for a meeting.

Selecting a chair person

The system of work described in this book is highly structured. Thus the planning work of the team needs to be properly organised. The role of the chair person in this is essential: the chair person's role is to keep team meetings task oriented, to see that everyone contributes to and participates in the decision making, and to ensure that clear decisions are actually made. This is a skilled job and should not be left to chance if the team is to function effectively. Rotating the chair round all the team members is not an appropriate solution. The chair person should be selected by the team members on the basis of his or her skills and personal qualities. He or she should be expected to serve in that capacity for at least a year; a deputy should also be selected to stand in during absences, and to take over if a limited 'term of office' is set.

Selecting a co-ordinator (key worker) for each client

If the team is working with a number of clients, then its functioning will be improved if each client has a co-ordinator (key worker). The role of the co-ordinator in the team is to lead the discussion on the client, collate all the necessary information and follow up the decisions made to see that they are carried out. There are other ways of fulfilling these functions, but vesting this in a single person who takes a special interest in the individual client is probably the most effective.

Selecting targets

All of the individuals with whom this book is concerned have multiple needs. If an agency is making plans for more than one individual, it becomes impossible to do everything that is needed for every person, so that some means of prioritising targets for intervention is needed. Otherwise team members may feel overwhelmed and/or discouraged. Two important guidelines for selecting targets can be offered. In the early stages always start with those individuals or programmes which are likely to have the greatest chance of success. This may mean *not* tackling straight away the problems held to be the most *critical*. It is important to break out from crisis thinking and reacting, as part of the move towards the longer term perspective advocated in this book. The second important guideline is always to start with positive programmes before beginning any negative programme.

Identifying responsibilities

Any programme must specify who is to carry out the programme (and when). This step, coupled to the specification of a review date (see earlier sections), will help to ensure that decisions made at meetings are put into practice.

Handling information

There should be one file for each client which deals with individual programming work. Such a file should contain all assessment information, all written programmes and all data analysis (such as graphs) and other charts. The individual record forms for skill teaching and problem behaviours may temporarily be stored in this file but should be destroyed as soon as the information has been analysed and summarised. Such a file should be purely for individual programme planning and separate from any more general record system. However, various parts of this information may be placed elsewhere in addition to the central file. For example, copies of programmes may be posted up to act as a reminder about programme details or to prompt programme implementation. Recording forms may likewise be posted up so that it is easy to record behaviour as and when it occurs. These are not alternatives to a proper filing system, however. There must always be one place to which people can go to find information on a client's achievements and needs, programmes which are being or have been done, and the effectiveness of these programmes.

Evaluating individual programmes

Built into the teamwork approach and the system of individual planning, with its data collection, is a means whereby rational judgements can be made as to whether programmes are working. Regular meetings and reviews are an essential part of quality control.

Evaluating the programme planning system

Review of the whole system of work should take place on a regular basis. In some settings this may be carried out by a line manager (for example, a head or deputy head teacher, or a manager of a day centre or residential home). However, many managers are not properly trained for this function, and difficulties arise when multiple agencies are involved.

A second approach is to employ independent external evaluators to 'audit' the system. However, access to such resources is rare. This means that in practice it is often down to those who run the system to try to do it for themselves. One way to do this is to set aside a specific meeting for this purpose. Such a meeting should include all those involved in the system and should occur on a regular, scheduled basis (for example, every six months or yearly). Its purpose is not to discuss individual programmes but to review the system of planning as a whole: how well do meetings and the information handling systems work, what proportion of programmes succeed, what support services are needed, what extra skills do staff need? Following the guidelines for individual planning itself, strengths of the system should be celebrated as well as needs being highlighted. Such a meeting may strengthen existing commitment and lead to improvements in both effectiveness and efficiency.

Ethical practice

There are a number of ways of providing the individual with an effective voice to ensure that his rights are protected.

Client involvement

Decision making about programmes should involve the client as much as possible. Some will be able to participate fully and need only the opportunity to do so. Others may need training to develop their participative skills (see below). Even a person whose contribution is difficult to elicit or understand can exert an influence by his physical presence. Simply having the person present when decisions are made will improve the quality of those decisions.

Client advocacy

It is essential for the client's views to be adequately represented. When the person can adequately represent himself, he needs only the opportunity. For children, parents or a legal guardian are held to be the legitimate advocate. Outside of these two examples, effective advocacy needs specific planning. Clients may be trained, either individually or with a group of others, to speak for themselves. Self-advocacy training is an important means of increasing control for the client. When this is not possible, then a system of independent advocacy will be helpful. Advocates should be 'lay' people, independent of the services and organisations working with the client. They should know the client well and seek to express the view of the client as they understand it. It may be difficult to obtain such advocates, but a number of organisations are now taking on the training and support of people for this role.

An ethical committee

Establishing an ethical committee will also help to maintain quality of work. The role of such a committee is to judge the acceptability of proposed programmes. It may review either all the programmes or only those brought forward as 'controversial'. It will work best where it meets regularly, is seen as an important part of the system of work, and has access to all information in the individual programme file (see above). Its composition should include senior professional staff, but the majority of members should be independent of the organisation(s) providing for the client. There should be representatives from parents' organisations, and membership should include one or more persons with a learning disability.

An ethical code

Drafting an ethical code is an important exercise in raising awareness of ethical issues and in providing detailed guidelines for every-day working practice. Such a code should be developed by the staff themselves in conjunction with an ethical committee (see above). It will need to cover the processes by which decisions are made: who speaks for the individual, who is consulted about programme content, whose agreement is necessary for a programme to be implemented, how unresolved conflicts should be handled. It will also offer specific guidelines about programme standards. For example, it can mandate skill building programmes to precede any aversive programmes. It can limit the intensity and duration of aversive procedures by, for example, limiting time-out or facial screening to a specific time period. It can also lay down other requirements relevant to good quality programming, such as requiring all staff to be trained in ethical issues or setting standards of competence before staff are permitted to design individual programmes. No code can hope to be comprehensive, but it will prove an invaluable source of guidance and protection for both staff and clients. It will take time to draft but it will work better if it is developed by those involved with the client than if some ready-made code is borrowed from elsewhere and imposed.

SUMMARY

Working with people who have severe learning disabilities and serious behaviour problems represents a challenge at many levels. It tests professional knowledge and understanding to its limits. It stretches and stresses resources, and increasingly highlights weaknesses in service systems. Yet so much *can* be achieved.

In this book an approach to understanding and interpreting behaviour difficulties has been offered. This approach has direct and immediate implications for what can be done in practice to help overcome these difficulties. Many techniques have been described, with a system for planning and implementing these techniques on an individual basis. Throughout there has been an emphasis upon a long-term perspective. Complex behavioural difficulties cannot be rapidly eliminated once and for all. A more patient, sustained approach is necessary, and consideration has been given to organisational factors which will help to implement and sustain constructive work. The ethics of intervention are the final and critical set of issues that have been discussed. For people as 'vulnerable' as the individuals with whom this book is concerned, there can never be too much care in the protection of their dignity and rights.

Working with people who have severe learning and behavioural disabilities is a complex enterprise. Complex but manageable. Making progress with such people is a long-term enterprise. Long term but achievable. In this book a model has been presented for analysing and intervening with problem behaviours at several levels. There is no doubt that if people can increase their understanding of the factors that lead to behaviour problems in people with severe learning disabilities and develop their skills in behaviour management, then significant headway can be made with the behavioural challenges of their clients. There is every reason to be optimistic.

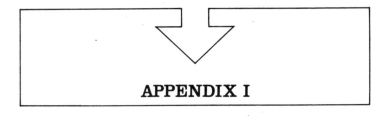

APPENDIX I

Case Examples

CAROL

Carol, a 23-year-old woman living on a 24-bedded ward in a long-stay mental handicap hospital, had been resident there since the age of six years. She had been admitted because of 'severe behaviour problems' making her 'unmanageable' at home. The ward was mixed sex with dormitories divided into individual cubicles. All residents were regarded as behaviourally disturbed. At any one time there would usually be one qualified nurse and three or four nursing assistants on duty. Carol attended no day facility but was taken out for walks in the hospital grounds and on occasional off-campus group outings. She was visited two or three times a year by her sister. The problem behaviour of concern was Carol's biting of other residents. This was of low frequency (five or six times a month) but high cost (the bites were usually on the cheek next to the eye). It had been a problem for many years but was getting worse. It was felt that if progress could not be made, Carol's teeth would have to be removed.

Establishing the team

A system of individual planning was introduced for all residents on the ward. Following discussions at senior management level in the hospital, the ward was assigned sessions of occupational therapy and clinical psychology time. A weekly team meeting was established, incorporating ward staff at all levels, the occupational therapist, the clinical psychologist, and the consultant psychiatrist. Each resident on the ward was assigned a key worker from among the unqualified nursing staff. At each weekly meeting a small number of residents were discussed and specific individual goals were reviewed.

Assessment

A skills checklist was completed and information was collected on Carol's likes and dislikes. An analysis was carried out of the problem behaviour using observation and interview techniques. This assessment suggested the following analysis of the biting.

Settings. The ward setting was relatively unstructured. Biting seemed more likely to occur when Carol had nothing to do, when there was a lot of noise or when changes occurred (for example, new staff). It also seemed more likely when she was agitated.

Triggers. No specific triggers could be identified.

Results. When a bit incident occurred, staff tended to run over to Carol, shouting. She was then held down, given an injection and sent to bed. It was felt that she used biting to gain attention when bored and to escape from unpleasant situations (noises, new people).

From the assessment, a strengths and needs list was compiled (Table AI.1).

Intervention

Teaching new skills

To work on her communication, Carol was seen for short, daily, individual sessions. The learning need identified in her strengths and needs list was translated into the following long-term goal: 'Carol will use Makaton signs to request favourite objects with prompting.' This was broken down into a series of short-term objectives, which included:

(a) learning motor imitation skills;
(b) labelling three objects using appropriate Makaton signs;
(c) requesting three objects using appropriate Makaton sign.

Error-free teaching procedures were used. Smarties cut in half were used to reinforce correct responses.

Table Al.1: Strengths and needs list, Carol

Strengths	Needs
Mobile	To stop biting other people
Understands instructions in every-day situations	To do things more with other people
Will usually take self to toilet and remains clean and dry	To learn an effective means of communication
Will help with domestic chores (e.g. tidying up)	
Feeds self with spoon	
Likes tea	
Likes sweets	
Sometimes smiles	
Can give a kiss on the cheek if requested	
Likes going for walks	
Has a good relationship with staff	
Likes curling up on a comfortable chair	
Likes quiet places	
Likes to spend time on her own	
Likes raisins	
Works best when given one-to-one attention	

Enhancing existing skills

Opportunities. Carol was given the opportunity of helping with domestic chores twice a day. Craft materials similar to those used in occupational therapy were made available for use on days when Carol could not go to OT. Each sequence of domestic chores was followed by a cup of tea.

Existing skills. For good behaviour (every hour when no biting occurred) Carol was given a raisin and a fuss was made of her.

Managing the problem behaviour

Settings. To increase structure and occupation, a regular timetable of activities was drawn up for Carol. The occupational therapist agreed to take her to the Department for three small-group craft sessions a week. To improve her mood, daily walks were introduced plus extra time with staff. A side room was equipped with a carpet and easy chair and its door was left open in case Carol should need somewhere quiet to go.

Triggers. Although no clear trigger for biting had been identified, Carol was warned verbally or with picture sequences of impending changes in the ward routine (staff or activities).

Results. If biting occurred, she was held by the shoulders, told firmly 'No, that hurts . . .'. Then all attention was given to the victim. She was ignored for the next half hour (with careful observation to protect other residents), and all forms of material reward (except meals) were suspended for the next 3 hours.

Recording

The frequency of biting was recorded on a continuous schedule, a 4-week baseline having been taken before the start of the programme. During individual skill teaching session, progress in skill learning was recorded separately.

Ethical considerations

Carol's problem had previously been discussed at the hospital's Controversial Treatment Committee, a multidisciplinary group of senior staff set up for consultation over methods used with difficult residents. Carol had been discussed when the issue had been the removal of her teeth, and the Committee had recommended further efforts at a more constructive approach with extra resources to be allocated to the ward. The programme outlined above was referred as a matter of course to this committee, who approved it on the understanding that meals would not be used as part of contingency management.

Outcome

Over a period of 12 months, Carol became more generally co-operative, regularly completing chores and participating in most activities offered. She smiled more. She made progress on imitation skills and could use three Makaton signs (drink, biscuit, sweet) with considerable prompting, but not spontaneously. The biting declined over the first 12 months and remained at zero level thereafter.

PHILIP

Philip was a large 14-year-old boy with Down's syndrome. He lived at home with his parents, attending a day school for children with severe learning difficulties. He spent one weekend a month at a local

189

residential unit. His behaviour had always been difficult to manage: he was disruptive in school, would frequently abscond when out, would sit down on the floor and refuse to move whenever asked to go to new activities or to get on to the school bus. These behaviours had been tolerated when he was smaller, but now he had become too large and heavy to be carried or physically prompted to stand up. Over the last year he had, in addition, become aggressive towards children and staff in school and even to strangers when out. Aggression would take the form of 'strangulating' his victim. This behaviour was frightening for all concerned. Philip was declared 'a problem' by his school, following a series of aggressive attacks in the playground.

Establishing the team

A new team was formed which consisted of Philip's class teacher, the classroom assistant, the family social worker, his key worker from the residential unit and the head teacher. Philip's parents, whilst admitting to problems with his behaviour at home, decided not to participate in the programme but readily gave their consent to a programme being set up at school and in the residential unit. Programme planning meetings for Philip were held weekly at school for the first 2 months. After this time, this was reduced to fortnightly. After 6 months, reviews continued to be held monthly.

Assessment

Over a 4-week period a full assessment was carried out of aggressive behaviour, a summary of Philip's skills was prepared and an assessment of motivators was carried out. Assessment of the problem behaviour suggested that aggression occurred in the following circumstances.

Settings. Aggression occurred mostly during unstructured times, such as playtimes. It also occurred during change (for example, changing from one activity to another) and in group settings, particularly when Philip had to spend a lot of time waiting to take a turn at an activity.

Triggers. No specific trigger was identified. It was noted, however, that he would always look towards an adult before an outburst of aggression.

Results. One result which Philip seemed to obtain from his aggressive (and non-compliant) behaviour was a good deal of

190

attention. Aggression inevitably resulted in three or four members of staff converging on Philip, shouting at him to release his victim and physically struggling with him to prise him off the victim. He would always laugh during this procedure. Another function which aggression seemed to serve was escape. Philip was dragged, or otherwise removed, from the situation and taken to an empty classroom with a member of staff, where he either worked or played alone with this member of staff for at least an hour. It was admitted by all concerned that Philip enjoyed these sessions.

From the assessment, the strengths and needs list shown in Table AI.2 was compiled.

Table AI.2: Strengths and needs list, Philip

Strengths	Needs
Occupies himself for long periods when alone	To stop being aggressive
Works well with individual attention	To comply with requests
Has a sense of humour	To learn to play interactive games with other children
Has good imaginative play skills	To be given more interesting and adult activities to do
Makes needs understood using words and signs	To be friendly towards other children more often
Understands short, simple phrases	
Enjoys jigsaws	
Enjoys creative work	
Enjoys playing alone in doll's house	
Can count to ten	
Can identify a few written words	
Can write his name	
Can be friendly to other children	
Can dress himself	
Feeds independently	
Dry by night and by day	
Likes trampolining	
Likes swimming	
At school, his behaviour can be easily controlled by the head teacher, deputy head and Chris	

Intervention

Teaching new skills

From the teaching needs identified above, the following goal was set at a long-term teaching objective: 'Philip will play ball games with other children in the playground.' (This skill was particularly related to one of the settings in which problems occurred.) This long-term goal was broken down into the following component skills:

(a) to kick a ball back and forth with another child;
(b) to invite other children to play ball with him.

These skills were taught using demonstration and role play, first indoors during specific sessions, then outdoors, when the playground was empty. The game itself was reinforcing for Philip. However, praise was also given for appropriate play during teaching sessions. The final stage in the teaching programme was to introduce other children into the teaching sessions, and to carry out these sessions during natural playtimes, when other children were present.

Enhancing existing skills

Opportunities. To increase his sense of responsibility and to provide him with more 'adult' activities, Philip was given important tasks to do around the school. He was made Register Monitor, and he was also made responsible for handing out milk to the children at drinks time.

Existing skills. Good behaviour (compliance, non-aggression) was praised on a frequent but informal basis. Praise was accompanied by specific feedback ('You have been good because . . .'). In particular, whenever Philip was seen being friendly towards other children he was given a lot of attention and a fuss was made of him. At the end of each morning and afternoon, if no aggression or non-compliance had occurred, he was allowed to choose a favourite play activity which he was allowed to do for 15 minutes.

Managing the problem behaviour

Settings. Philip's day was structured so that identified 'problem' situations where aggression might occur were avoided. He was kept back from school outings, and from going out into the playground. In the mornings he was met off the bus and taken to a separate room till the other children from his class had settled. He was taken to each new activity (lunch, school bus, hall, etc.) ahead of the other children. Philip was gradually reintroduced to the natural settings as his programme progressed.

Triggers. Philip was taught, using correspondence training, to provide himself with cues for appropriate behaviour in each of the settings from which he had been withdrawn. This was done using pictorial sequences of 'appropriate' behaviours for each situation. These sequences were demonstrated and practised in role play. A graded approach was used. Thus, one situation was taken at a time. He was exposed to each situation for gradually longer periods of time, to maximise the opportunity of his behaving appropriately (for example, he was introduced to playtimes first for 5 minutes, then 10, then 15, then for the whole playtime).

Results. Refusing to go from one activity to another was responded to by telling him once only that he was 'silly'. He was asked once only to comply, then he was left where he was, without attention or activities, until he joined the group. Aggression was responded to with one firm warning to stop. If he persisted, one of three members of staff who had been identified previously as having control over Philip's behaviour (this avoided the need for two or three adults to physically prompt him to comply) was called to take Philip to stand outside the head teacher's office for 5 minutes (he found this particularly aversive).

Recording

Aggression was recorded throughout the school day. Non-compliance was also recorded throughout the day. Friendly approaches to other children were recorded each Friday during lunch, and specific recording was carried out during skill teaching sessions.

Ethical considerations

Philip's parents were consulted at each stage of the programme and their consent was obtained for all aspects of the programme prior to implementation. They were kept informed of progress by the social worker.

Outcome

Tension over Philip's behaviour decreased early during the

193

programme when settings were restructured to avoid aggressive behaviours. This allowed Philip to receive more positive responses from his teachers. As a result his compliance increased. It took three months to reintroduce Philip to his first 'problem' setting — the playground. After this, however, he progressed faster, so that within six months he was participating in all his class activities, both in and out of school. A high rate of positive reinforcement for existing skills continued for a further month, before being systematically phased out. Interactive skills continued to be taught over the whole year. He learned to play and initiate ball games and games of 'He', and to race tricycles appropriately with other children. Indoors, he learned to play simple card games, such as 'Snap'. He was taught to involve other children in his imaginative games. Correspondence training was introduced to the residential unit during the fourth month of the programme. His behaviour improved there as well. At home, his behaviour remained unchanged and he continued to be difficult with his parents.

PETER

Peter was a 12-year-old boy with Down's syndrome who lived at home with his mother, attending a school for children with severe learning difficulties by day and a short-stay residential unit for one week every month. The problem behaviour, which had developed over the last few years, was 'twiddling'. He would spend every available moment of the day twiddling any object that came to hand. He was therefore continually holding some object and engrossed in watching it. The behaviour was quite compulsive. He would frequently knock things over as he walked past, in order to watch them spinning on the floor. This included glasses from the dinner table, flower pots, etc. He would even upturn rubbish bins to watch the bin spinning and then would pick up each object and twiddle it before replacing it back in the bin. It was very difficult to interrupt this behaviour: Peter would become agitated and start to make a loud wailing noise. Both his mother and his class teacher found the behaviour distressing and disruptive. Peter needed to be watched constantly to prevent him destroying property. It was felt, too, that the behaviour was preventing him using his hands in more constructive activities and impeding his further development.

The team

Regular meetings were set up between Peter's mother, his class teacher, a speech therapist and his key worker from the residential unit. Meetings were held monthly at the school. The head teacher and a clinical psychologist were involved in the initial planning meeting where it was agreed to undertake what would be expected to be long-term and intensive work, which might require extra staff input at school. The psychologist remained available for consultation to the team throughout the programme.

Assessment

The assessment of the problem behaviour was carried out in all three settings (home, school, residential unit) and this information was collated by one named member of the team. A summary of his skills was drawn up and motivators were established during a team discussion.

Assessment of the problem behaviour yielded the following information.

Settings. Twiddling and throwing could occur in any situation, regardless of what activities were in progress or how structured or calm the situations were. It would occur both indoors and outdoors. Twiddling was the only activity in which he would voluntarily engage.

Triggers. The triggers were too many to name. All small moveable objects were a potential target for twiddling or throwing. It was observed that Peter would often look towards his mother or teacher just before picking up a new object to twiddle or throw and wait till their backs were turned before picking it up.

Results. Twiddling and throwing seemed to be a major source of occupation for Peter. He would often pick noisy objects to twiddle, spin or throw and seemed to enjoy the auditory stimulation which these provided. He would watch objects intently as they spun. Sometimes he would put them to his face or mouth as they spun and appeared to gain tactile stimulation from them also.

From the comprehensive assessment the strengths and needs list shown in Table AI.3 was produced.

195

Table AI.3: Strengths and needs list, Peter

Strengths	Needs
Co-operates with dressing	To reduce twiddling
Can pull up pants and trousers	To stop throwing
Feeds himself with a spoon	To communicate his needs
Will hold fork/knife in other hand and use if reminded	To increase range of activities he likes to do
Drinks from a cup	To be more sociable
Goes to toilet if reminded	
Opens bowels on toilet	
Understands a few simple instructions	
Can scribble with crayon	
Will carry empty cup into kitchen on request	
Likes being outdoors	
Likes watching people/activities in progress	
Likes watching football on TV	
Likes being alone	
Likes milk	
Likes fruit salad	
Likes walking to and from the shops	
Likes twiddling	
Likes to have his hair ruffled	
Concentrates on tasks for up to 3 minutes	
Responds to a sharp 'No'	
Will go up to his mother for a cuddle	

Intervention

Teaching new skills

Regular individual sessions were set up by the speech therapist to develop Peter's communication skills. One long-term goal was 'Peter will make choices when offered two alternative activities.' Prerequisite skills which had to be taught were *attending* to what was being presented, and *co-operating* with the session.

His class teacher set up specific teaching sessions to teach him skills which were incompatible with twiddling (for example, water play, drawing, pushing toys on wheels). In all cases, error-free techniques were used, his teacher using pieces of fruit salad as a reinforcer for correct responding.

Enhancing existing skills

Peter was encouraged at home to engage in as many domestic activities with his mother as possible. She encouraged him to fetch and carry, and to 'help' to do the washing up and tidying.

At school and at home, whenever he was observed to engage in *any* activity other than twiddling or throwing, he was given attention and physical contact.

Managing the problem behaviour

Settings. No changes were made to settings.

Triggers. Since twiddling was his major source of occupation, it was felt to be inappropriate to try to prevent twiddling altogether. It was decided, however, to gain greater control over the triggers for twiddling, in particular to narrow these down. In each of the three settings where change was to occur (home, school, residential unit), two toys were designated as 'permitted twiddlers'. These were always made available and he was encouraged and praised for using these. An informal but highly frequent schedule of reinforcement was used.

Results. Whenever he was seen to twiddle any object other than a permitted twiddler or to throw an object, this was responded to by the adult cupping Peter's face in his hands, drawing his face close to Peter's, saying firm, 'No, Peter, that's naughty', and continuing to stare at him from this close distance for a slow count of five. (This response was first practised during role-play sessions.) The object was then removed from Peter.

This part of the programme was carried out initially at home, during the school holidays. Here it was done consistently throughout the day. At the start of the new term, it was introduced at school — first on a sessional basis (up to an hour a day according to staffing levels). At the residential unit, it tended to be done only when the key worker was on duty. At both school and the residential unit, it was felt to be unsatisfactory to carry out the programme intermittently. Extra staff were made available at school and the programme was extended throughout the day.

A problem developed with the programme when Peter learned to 'twiddle' his permitted twiddler with one hand while twiddling or throwing other objects with the free hand. The programme was modified to deal with this problem. The 'eyeballing' procedure

197

described above was followed by removal of both twiddlers (including the permitted one) and Peter was made to sit on a chair without attention or activities for one minute.

Recording

The total duration of twiddling was recorded over a half-hour period each day. Each incident requiring 'eyeballing' was recorded.

Outcome

Peter learned to discriminate between permitted and non-permitted twiddlers quite quickly. Within 4 months of the start of the programme he was twiddling only permitted twiddlers in all settings. A positive side-effect of this intervention was that he became more agreeable to giving up his permitted twiddlers during individual sessions. As a result he appeared more relaxed during these and began to be more co-operative and to participate more in them. He learned to make choices within these sessions. This generalised to his choosing his drinks or foods whenever possible. At home, he began to use his existing skills more frequently, and became more interested generally in his environment. Progress was slowest at the residential unit where it took a longer time for Peter to learn to give up his permitted twiddlers on request.

After 7 months, permitted twiddlers began to be gradually phased out, on a session-by-session basis. At the end of 1 year he was twiddling only for very short periods of the day. He had become more socially responsive, smiled more often and appeared much happier. His mother was able to leave him unattended in a room without worrying that he would break objects. At school, he began to participate more in group activities. Sessional skill teaching continued for a further 6 months, during which time the problem did not recur.

CHRISTINE

Christine was a 7-year-old girl living at home with her mother and attending a special school for children with severe learning difficulties. She was intellectually impaired by encephalitis at the age of 8 months, and problems with her hips had required surgical intervention which meant that she could no longer bear weight through her legs. She could sit up unaided and roll, but she could not crawl. She was moved around in a wheelchair. She could see and hear, but the acuity of her sensory systems had been difficult to establish with any precision.

The problem with which she presented was head banging (head to arm resting on a solid surface, or bringing her arm up to strike her head). This had been present in her repertoire since 2 years of age, but had been perceived as getting worse. It was a low-intensity but very high-frequency behaviour, which had produced a large marked area on her forehead, and one agency had prescribed a protective helmet for Christine. If left unchecked she could bang several thousand times in an hour.

The team

Christine was admitted to a special intensive treatment unit where there was a multidisciplinary team which held weekly goal planning meetings on each of its clients. Thus, the core team was already established with its own structural framework. Christine's parents and school were considered to be an essential part of the team and were invited to as many planning meetings as they were able to attend.

Assessment

A developmental checklist was completed. Information about motivators was obtained through interviewing those who knew her best and from direct observation of Christine on the Unit.

The problem behaviour was assessed by interview and observation, including some observation sessions specifically structured to look at factors that influenced the frequency of head banging (for example, in the absence of toys, continued attention, no attention). From this assessment the following relevant factors emerged:

Settings. Banging was more likely to occur when Christine was tired or generally miserable. Her sleep pattern was such that she took many, very short sleeps in the day. It was more likely when her arms were free to move and when there were surfaces on which her arms could rest and which reverberated.

Triggers. The banging itself appeared to trigger Christine falling asleep. Thus fatigue could trigger the banging itself. Banging could be triggered by the presence of surfaces as described and sometimes by task demands (especially when Christine was tired).

Results. Banging appeared to achieve the onset of sleep and escape from demands when tired. It also achieved certain kinds of sensory

199

Table AI.4: Strengths and needs list, Christine

Strengths	Needs
Smiles	To bang her head less often
Communicates happiness or sadness by identifiable vocalisations and changes in facial expression	To play more constructively
	To get a more regular sleep pattern
Holds toys	
Lifts hand to mouth	
Will explore objects with her hands and mouth	
Likes banging noises	
Chews solid food	
Likes to out in the open air	
Sits in chair	
Lifts head when placed over wedge	
Rolls off a wedge	
Is very popular with staff	
Reaches for objects shown to her	
Likes vibrating objects	

stimulation (auditory or vibratory).

From the overall assessment, the strength and needs list shown in Table AI.4 was compiled.

Intervention

Enhancing existing skills

In order to maintain sensory stimulation skills, a timetable was drawn up which changed Christine's position and the materials available to her every 15 minutes during the school day. All materials could be actively used by Christine. An attempt to use differential reinforcement for periods of not banging was made, using vibration delivered through a specially constructed chair. This was not effective and so was abandoned.

Teaching new skills

Specific training was conducted on a sessional basis to teach Christine to use a specific noise-making toy (banging one thing with another). Error-free teaching procedures were used.

Managing the problem behaviour

Settings. In order to maintain a reasonable mood level, Christine's timetable was structured to include a lot of pleasurable activities (for example, walks out). Her sleep pattern was restructured to avoid the frequent onset of fatigue. She was specifically encouraged to sleep at a set time in the day (between 12.30 and 1.30 p.m.). She was settled using the same routine as her mother used to settle her at night. A tape of a metronome was played during settling to try to substitute for banging against the pillow. She was actively prevented from sleeping at all other times in the day.

Triggers. This was tackled in part through the sleep programme. The use of sensory materials (see above) was to trigger alternative ways of gaining sensory stimulation.

Results. Whenever Christine banged, she was told 'No' sharply and her hands were held down on to her lap from behind for 5 seconds. This was begun in her daily half-hour sessions and generalised as success was achieved. Her helmet was kept for use at times when she could not be closely supervised.

Recording

Frequency of head banging was monitored using sampling techniques. Recording was carried out each day, at a preset time, for half an hour. Christine's sleep pattern was recorded daily.

Ethical considerations

The Unit had a written ethical code of practice which had been followed at all stages of the programme. It included procedures for obtaining consent, for limiting the use of aversive procedures and for mandating alternative skill teaching as part of the overall management programme. The programme was presented to an ethical committee and reviewed by this committee every 2 months.

Outcome

Initial assessment took 2 months, and implementation and refinement of the programme over the next 6 months led to a major decrease in the frequency of banging (but not total elimination). Christine's sleep pattern became more stable around the new routines, and her mood remained generally good (with some

201

variability). She began to respond to the warning signal ('No'), by stopping banging — the first clear indication of any response to a word. Little progress in terms of mastery of new play skills was achieved, but progress in self-feeding skills was made. The helmet was not needed. Nine months later this degree of progress had been maintained despite changes in day-care staff and settings.

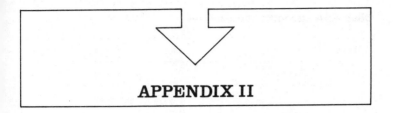

APPENDIX II

Sample Recording Charts

Chart 1: A STAR recording chart

Name				
Behaviour to be Observed				
Date	Setting	Trigger	Action	Result

Chart 2: A strengths and needs list

Name	Date
Strengths	Needs

Chart 3: A standard programme form

Name	Date
Long Term Goal	
Short Term Objective	
People Involved	
Time & Place	
Special Materials	Trials per Session
Procedure	
Response to Appropriate Behaviour	
Response to Inappropriate Behaviour	
Generalisation	
Recording	Date of review

APPENDIX III

Some Useful References Dealing with Skills Assessment Schedules

Bluma, S., Shearer, M., Froman, A. and Hilliard, J. (1976) *The Portage Guide to Early Education. Checklist.* The Portage Project, Cooperative Education Service Agency 12, 412 East Slifer Street, Portage, Wisconsin 53901, USA. Available in the UK from NFER–Nelson, Darville House, 2 Oxford Road East, Windsor, Berks. SL4 1DF, UK.

Gunzburg, H.C. (1977) *Progress Assessment Charts.* 4 Great William Street, Stratford-upon-Avon, Worcs, UK, *or* MENCAP Bookshop, 123 Golden Lane, London EC1V 0RT, UK. (No current US distributor.)

Jenkins, J., Felce, D. and Mansell, J. (1983) *The Bereweeke Skill Teaching System: Assessment Checklist.* NFER–Nelson Publishing Co., Darville House, 2 Oxford Road East, Windsor, Berks. SL4 1DF, UK (worldwide distributor).

Kiernan, C. and Jones, M. (1982) *Behaviour Assessment Battery.* NFER–Nelson Publishing Co., Darville House, 2 Oxford Road East, Windsor, Berks. SL4 1DF, UK (worldwide distributor).

Nihira, K., Foster, R., Shellhaas, M. and Leland, H. (1974) *AAMD Adaptive Behaviour Scale.* AAMD, 5101 Wisconsin Avenue NW, Washington, DC 20016, USA.

Williams, C. (1982) *The STAR Profile — Social Training Achievement Record.* BIMH Publications, Wolverhampton Road, Kidderminster, Worcs. DY10 2UT, UK.

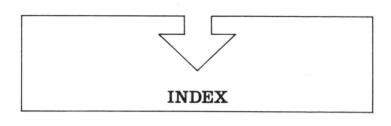

INDEX